Spiritual Gifts

Spiritual Gifts

A Christ-Centered Perspective

Jennifer Anne Cox

RESOURCE *Publications* · Eugene, Oregon

SPIRITUAL GIFTS
A Christ-Centered Perspective

Resource Publications
An Imprint of Wipf and Stock Publishers
199 W. 8th Ave., Suite 3
Eugene, OR 97401

www.wipfandstock.com

PAPERBACK ISBN: 978-1-5326-3592-2
HARDCOVER ISBN: 978-1-5326-3594-6
EBOOK ISBN: 978-1-5326-3593-9

Manufactured in the U.S.A.

"Now concerning spiritual gifts, brothers, I do not want you to be uninformed"
(1 Cor 12:1).

.

Contents

CONTENTS

Introduction

THIS BOOK IS THE fruit of a personal Bible study I conducted over the course of about a year. The original question I was exploring had to do with the sphere in which spiritual gifts belong—inside the church, in the world, or both. As I reflected on the biblical material pertaining to the question, it soon became evident that a there is a great deal to consider. Not only so, but I began to ask other questions. The result was a deep exploration of the gifts within the wider biblical perspective.

I have attempted to answer several different questions in this book. Although I began with asking where the gifts should be used, this is not the most important question. Theology must primarily be concerned to connect every topic to the center, namely, the Lord Jesus Christ. Consequently, the book explores spiritual gifts in the life of Jesus, how Jesus uses the gifts in his body (as exemplified in the early church), and how spiritual gifts are related to the gospel.

Unlike many books on spiritual gifts, this book does not provide a spiritual gifts test. It is not a series of stories about Christians using gifts in modern contexts. Instead, it seeks to provide a solid biblical foundation for the use of the gifts by the body of Christ. It begins with the wider context of spiritual gifts, by considering the work of the Holy Spirit and the nature of Christian ministry. There is a significant change in the presence of the Spirit from the Old Testament to the New and therefore a change in how ministry is done. With this foundation in place, I then work through what the New Testament has to say about spiritual gifts and their use. Then each gift is considered in turn. The book draws on the Gospel accounts of the life of Jesus, examples of gifts used in the book of Acts, and what the epistles tell us about each gift.

I hope that by reading this book, Christians may be encouraged to serve one another in the church through the use of the gifts of the Spirit, and to faithfully and effectively proclaim the gospel to the world, equipped with gifts given for the salvation of the lost.

Part 1

Context

1

The Holy Spirit in the Old Testament

Before we can possibly understand what the Holy Spirit is doing in the lives of believers by imparting *charismata* (grace gifts), we must understand who the Spirit himself is and what he does. For this we need to begin in the Old Testament. Entire books might be written simply on this topic alone. Therefore, this is but a summary of what the Old Testament has to say about the Spirit of God. The discussion is not intended to cover everything but is directed towards seeing how the Spirit works among the people of God.

"In the beginning, God created the heavens and the earth. The earth was without form and void, and darkness was over the face of the deep. And the Spirit of God was hovering over the face of the waters" (Gen 1:1–2). The Spirit hovered over the formless and empty world, waiting for the voice of the Father to speak so that he could bring the word of God into being. From the beginning, the Holy Spirit is connected with creation. He brings God's purposes to fruition. He makes the world what it is intended to be. Without the Spirit of God the will of God and his word would not bear fruit for God's glory.

The Spirit is even more intimately involved with the creation of humanity. All creatures are given life by the Holy Spirit (Ps 104:30), but the creature who is given life in the most personal way is the human. "Then the Lord God formed the man of dust from the ground and breathed into his nostrils the breath of life, and the man became a living creature" (Gen 2:7). By virtue of this act of giving life, humans have a relationship with the Holy Spirit. This does not necessarily provide assurance of sonship before God, but it is an inescapable relationship (Ps 139:7). The ongoing relationship between the Spirit and humanity implies that he is concerned with the lives and the plight of human creatures, whether they are Christian believers or not.

We can only speculate about what the relationship between the Holy Spirit and humans would have looked like if sin had not become part of the world. What we do know for sure is that the God who created human beings in his image and likeness did not abandon humanity to a life without relationship with God. But rather he chose people for himself. First God chose Abraham so that through him all the nations of the earth would be blessed (Gen 12:3; 18:18). The descendents of Abraham became the nation of Israel and in that nation the presence of the Holy Spirit was most felt. The Holy Spirit was present first in guiding the people as a nation and also present within certain individuals in Israel.

The people of Israel were brought out of Egypt by the power of the Holy Spirit. He was in their midst as they came through the Red Sea and brought them to a place of rest. He guided them and did miracles so that they would be delivered from bondage (Isa 63:10–14). The Holy Spirit continued to dwell in the midst of the nation of Israel (Hag 2:5). He was present to instruct that nation (Neh 9:20). This was, however, a presence for a nation not for individuals. The Spirit did not indwell all people. There were very few people privileged enough to personally experience the abiding presence of the Holy Spirit. God was active by his Spirit, but only a few select people could say that the Spirit was in them, and even then there was a real possibility that the Spirit would be removed.

The first person the Bible records as having the Spirit of God in him is Joseph (Gen 41:38). Pharaoh observed this because Joseph was able to interpret dreams and had great wisdom (Gen 41:15–36). The Holy Spirit indwelt Joseph in order to keep the people of God alive during a great famine. The next person mentioned who had the Spirit indwell him is Bezalel. He was filled with the Spirit so that he could make the tabernacle for worship (Exod 31:1–5). The building of the tabernacle was too important to be done in human ability alone; the people who built the tent in which worship and sacrifice took place needed to have the gifting of the Spirit.

But it is Moses who most typifies the anointing of the Spirit. Moses was called by the LORD to lead Israel out of Egypt. There is no mention of the Spirit upon Moses until Num 11. Yet prior to this time, Moses was plainly a man who heard the voice of God. This is the mark of a prophet. And in Num 11 this is made explicit.

> Then the LORD said to Moses, 'Gather for me seventy men of the elders of Israel, whom you know to be the elders of the people and officers over them, and bring them to the tent of meeting, and let them take their stand there with you. And I will come down and talk with you there. And I will take some of the Spirit that is on you and put it on them, and they shall bear the burden of the people with you, so that you may not bear it yourself alone' (Num 11:16–17).

Moses was able to lead Israel because the Spirit of God was upon him. If Moses were to have effective help in leading, then others would also need to be given the Spirit.

> So Moses went out and told the people the words of the LORD. And he gathered seventy men of the elders of the people and placed them around the tent. Then the LORD came down in the cloud and spoke to him, and took some of the Spirit that was on him and put it on the seventy elders. And as soon as the Spirit rested on them, they prophesied. But they did not continue doing it. Now two men remained in the camp, one named Eldad, and the other named Medad, and the Spirit rested on them. They were among those registered, but they had not gone out to the tent, and so they prophesied in the camp. And a young man ran and told Moses, 'Eldad and Medad are prophesying in the camp.' And Joshua the son of Nun, the assistant of Moses from his youth, said, 'My lord Moses, stop them.' But Moses said to him, 'Are you jealous for my sake? Would that all the LORD's people were prophets, that the LORD would put his Spirit on them!' (Num 11:24–29).

How rare it was for people to have the Spirit upon them and even rarer for the Spirit to dwell in someone permanently! The seventy men prophesied briefly and then did not prophesy again, since their gift of prophecy was only temporary. However, there is an indication that this situation would change in the future. Moses' statement, "Would that all the LORD's people were prophets, that the LORD would put his Spirit on them!" is prophetic. It looks forward to a time when God would pour out his Spirit on all his people. It expresses a desire in the heart of God.

There are a few other examples of people whom the Spirit anointed, some for a short time and others for longer. Balaam, who was employed by Balak to curse Israel, was briefly moved by the Spirit of God (Num 24:1–3). Joshua, who succeeded Moses, was given the Spirit (Num 27:18; Deut 34:9). The Spirit also empowered the judges of Israel to lead Israel and to overcome her enemies. The list includes Othniel (Judg 3:10), Gideon (Judg 6:34), Jephthah (Judg 11:29), and Samson (Judg 13:25; 14:6, 19; 15:14). In the case of Samson, the power of the Spirit was the cause of his great strength. But the writer explicitly states that the Spirit departed from Samson (Judg 16:20). The work of the Spirit in the judges was limited. They did not prophesy, there was little sanctification, and the anointing of the Spirit was temporary, since the Spirit was given only for the purpose of defeating physical enemies.

In the case of some kings, there is specific mention that the Spirit was upon them. When the first king—Saul—was chosen, the Spirit of God came upon him in power and he prophesied (1 Sam 10:6, 9–11). However, when Saul was disobedient to the commands of Yahweh, the Spirit left him (1 Sam 16:14). King David was given the Spirit (1 Sam 16:13). He is considered a prophet (rather than one who just occasionally prophesied as Saul did). David said, "The Spirit of the LORD speaks by me; his word is on my tongue" (2 Sam 23:2). And yet even David considered it possible that the Holy Spirit might be taken away from him (Ps 51:11).

Prophets in particular experienced the anointing of the Spirit. Elijah and Elisha are good examples. Elijah was carried along by the Holy Spirit (1 Kgs 18:12) and Elisha walked in the footsteps of Elijah since he had a double portion of Elijah's spirit (2 Kgs 2:9). Both prophets did many miraculous things as well as being spokesmen for the Spirit. Elijah multiplied the oil and flour of the widow of Zarephath (1 Kgs 17) and called down fire on a sacrifice on Mt Carmel (1 Kgs 18). Elisha did more miracles than his predecessor did: making water safe (2 Kgs 2:19–22); multiplying a widow's oil (2 Kgs 4:1–7); giving a son to a barren woman and later raising him from the dead (2 Kgs 4:8–37); feeding a hundred people with twenty loaves (2 Kgs 4:42–44); healing an Aramean of leprosy (2 Kgs 5); and making an axe-head float (2 Kgs 6:1–7). Elisha could also see into the spiritual realm and caused the army of Aram to be blinded (2 Kgs 6:8–23).

There is not much evidence that priests had the Holy Spirit upon them. However, when the priests were consecrated they were anointed with oil (Exod 28:41; 29:7; Lev 8:30). This is evocative of the anointing of the Holy Spirit. The anointing oil was made of a special blend of spices, was only used for sacred purposes, and was not to touch anyone who was not a priest (Exod 30:25–32). The task of priests was an intercessory one, bringing sacrifices from the people to God. It would not be surprising if this work needed the presence of the Spirit. There is one example of a priest being "clothed" with the Spirit of God and who then acted as a prophet (2 Chr 24:20).

The written prophets also experienced the anointing of the Holy Spirit. Ezekiel mentions this several times. "As he spoke to me, the Spirit entered into me and set me on my feet, and I heard him speaking to me" (Ezek 2:2; see also 3:24; 11:5). It is clear that Ezekiel and the other written prophets were able to hear God speak his word, and subsequently proclaim that word, because they were anointed by the Holy Spirit.

The written prophets pointed forward to a time when a Savior would come, who would be filled with the Spirit, and a time when all God's people would be indwelt by the Holy Spirit. The clearest prediction about the Messiah being anointed by the Holy Spirit is found in Isaiah.

> And the Spirit of the LORD shall rest upon him, the Spirit of wisdom and understanding, the Spirit of counsel and might, the Spirit of knowledge and the fear of the LORD. And his delight shall be in the fear of the LORD. He shall not judge by what his eyes see, or decide disputes by what his ears hear, but with righteousness he shall judge the poor, and decide with equity for the meek of the earth; and he shall strike the earth with the rod of his mouth, and with the breath of his lips he shall kill the wicked (Isa 11:2–4).

The servant anointed by the Spirit is mentioned again in Isa 42:1 and Isa 61:1. The New Testament understands that these promises are about Jesus Christ. Because the Messiah is filled with the Holy Spirit, he will bring justice to the poor, and healing to the sick and broken-hearted. The captives will be set free. Even the nations will receive blessing because of him.

The overflow of the Messiah's anointing with the Spirit will be that the Spirit is poured out on all God's people.

> And it shall come to pass afterward, that I will pour out my Spirit on all flesh; your sons and your daughters shall prophesy, your old men shall dream dreams, and your young men shall see visions. Even on the male and female servants in those days I will pour out my Spirit (Joel 2:28–29).

> And I will give you a new heart, and a new spirit I will put within you. And I will remove the heart of stone from your flesh and give you a heart of flesh. And I will put my Spirit within you, and cause you to walk in my statutes and be careful to obey my rules (Ezek 36:26–27).

The Holy Spirit has been at work in humanity since the creation of the world. As the Lord and giver of life, he is vitally connected to human beings. His work in people was concentrated in those called by God to be his covenant people, the nation of Israel. The Spirit was actively involved in delivering Israel from Egypt and working among them as a nation. Yet only a few people were indwelt by the Holy Spirit under the old covenant. In the main, these were kings and prophets. But the Old Testament points forward to a time when the Messiah, and those who believe in him, would be filled with the Spirit and indwelt by him permanently. There is a profound difference between the presence of the Spirit in the Old Testament and the New. This has significant consequences for the way in which God works through his people, as we will see in the next chapter.

2

Paradigms for Ministry

THERE ARE MANY DIFFERENCES between the old covenant and the new. One that is directly related to spiritual gifts is the difference in paradigms for ministry. Ministry under the old covenant was centered on a few key people. But ministry under the new covenant is conducted by every member of the household of God.

The scarcity of people indwelt and anointed by the Spirit directly relates to the paradigm for ministry we find in the Old Testament. This paradigm is evident in the lives of Israel's prophets, particularly Moses, Elijah, and Elisha. Moses was Israel's greatest prophet because he gave them the law. But Moses also did a lot of other wonderful things. He heard directly from God (Exod 3; 33:11), rather than in indirect ways like other prophets (Num 12:6–8). Moses did many miracles: inflicting plagues on Egypt (Exod 7–11); parting the Red Sea (Exod 14:6); and getting water from the rock (Exod 17:6). He healed Miriam of leprosy (Num 12:13). He judged disputes and made decisions for the people (Exod 18:13), and later shared this job with others. He interceded for the people so that God would not kill them (Exod 32). In Moses we find a leader who did almost everything, and consequently the people relied on Moses to mediate for them, rather than having a direct relationship with God themselves.

Elijah and Elisha also present a paradigm for ministry (see 1 Kgs 17–19 and 2 Kgs 2–8, 13). They were the super prophets. Elijah challenged the prophets of Baal and called down fire from heaven. Elisha healed poisoned water, made an axe-head float, produced endless oil for a widow, healed other prophets, healed leprosy, raised the dead, and saw angelic armies.

They both heard directly from God and called people to repentance. They both had supernatural authority. Elijah and Elisha were seemingly able to do everything. They had multiple spiritual gifts when other people had none.

However, these Old Testament examples are not a paradigm for New Testament ministry. The Holy Spirit was given to very few people under the old covenant. Therefore, a very select group of people were given many gifts for the sake of the few. Ministry gifts lay with certain leaders and none other. This in some ways parallels the priesthood. Under the old covenant only particular men from one tribe (Levites) and descended from one man (Aaron) could offer sacrifices to God. It was unacceptable for others to do this. Even kings could not offer incense on the altar (2 Chr 26). We should not transpose old covenant conditions onto the new covenant since this will distort the gospel.

Unfortunately, the old covenant paradigm for ministry, exemplified in Moses, Elisha, and Elijah, is actually quite common in churches. The expectation is that a few people—Christian leaders, pastors, or priests—are paid to minister. They are expected to do everything—to lead, to decide what the Bible says, to communicate with God, and give answers from God. Most Christians do not expect their leaders to heal the sick or do miracles because there is little expectation that these things will happen. But in general, paid leaders are expected to do ministry on behalf of us all. The result of this wrong paradigm is a passive church that does not minister effectively because Christians believe that ministry is the job of a professional. This is by no means the New Testament picture.

One would be wrong to assume that the ministry paradigm that Jesus exemplified is again one in which one person has all the gifts and does all the work. It is true that Christian ministry must begin with the one man, Jesus, because he is the first to be fully anointed by the Spirit and have the Spirit remain on him (John 1:32–33). The work of the Holy Spirit must necessarily begin in Jesus and be completed in him before it can be done in his people. It is only because of his life, death, and resurrection that we are able to have a share in the Holy Spirit (e.g., John 7:39). Even so, while Jesus was still on the earth he began to train his disciples to do the work that he was doing.

Matthew and Mark record Jesus sending out the twelve to join in his work. "And he called to him his twelve disciples and gave them authority over unclean spirits, to cast them out, and to heal every disease and every affliction" (Matt 10:1; see also Mark 6:7). Luke records Jesus sending out an even larger group. "After this the Lord appointed seventy-two others and sent them on ahead of him, two by two, into every town and place where he himself was about to go" (Luke 10:1). The idea of the disciples sharing in the work of Jesus is expressed differently in John. "We must work the works of him who sent me while it is day; night is coming, when no one can work" (John 9:4). The disciples along with Jesus—*we*—were called to do the work of God. So even during the time Jesus was walking the earth, he expanded his ministry to include his disciples.

In the book of Acts, the ministry is at first carried out by the apostles. They had a particular calling to be witnesses to the risen Jesus, to proclaim the word that they alone knew. But this situation, in which the apostles were the only ones doing the ministry, was not satisfactory for long. In Acts 6, a situation arose in the church that needed attention. The apostles could not deal with it because they still had to give themselves to the proclamation of the word (v. 2). So deacons were appointed to distribute food to the widows in the church (vv. 1–4). But the work of the deacons was more than administrative. Stephen, one of the deacons, was soon preaching the word himself and doing miracles (vv. 8–10). After Stephen was martyred, the church in Jerusalem experienced persecution and were scattered all through Judea and Samaria (Acts 8:1). This had the effect of opening up ministry to the whole church. "Now those who were scattered went about preaching the word" (Acts 8:4). Thus the work of God began with the apostles but expanded to include every believer.

Neither the unique nature of Jesus nor the special calling of the apostles leads me to believe that New Testament ministry is given to only a few. Indeed, the opposite is true. New Testament ministry is entrusted to the whole church. "And he [Christ] gave the apostles, the prophets, the evangelists, the shepherds and teachers, *to equip the saints for the work of ministry*, for building up the body of Christ, until we all attain to the unity of the faith and of the knowledge of the Son of God, to mature manhood, to the measure of the stature of the fullness of Christ" (Eph 4:11–13). Rather than a ministry paradigm that has a select few people doing all the work for God, this passage offers a different understanding of ministry. Jesus, when he ascended to the right hand of God, gave gifts to his church. In this instance, the gifts are people whose task it is to provide leadership. But it is not the task of leaders to do the work of ministry. Instead, their task is to equip (that is, bring to a place of complete preparedness) the whole body of Christ to do the work of ministry.

While we continue to think of ministry as something done by a few people who are paid to engage in it, then spiritual gifts will be seen as optional to the Christian life. At best, according to the false paradigm of the ministry of the few, spiritual gifts might get an airing for a few minutes on a Sunday morning. This would make the study of spiritual gifts something quaint and possibly esoteric but not something that actually matters to Christians, expect for a select few. This is far from the expectation of the New Testament. Since the whole body of Christ is to be equipped for the work of ministry, the whole body of Christ must understand spiritual gifts. The topic of spiritual gifts is important to every Christian because we are each engaged in Christian ministry.

But lest readers of this statement assume that all Christians must somehow find a place within the church to minister, it needs to be emphasized that Christian ministry is intended to flow beyond the borders of the church in order to impact the world around us. Those who follow Jesus are *sent out* to do the work. The first disciples were called by Jesus and told, "Follow me, and I will make you fishers of men" (Matt 4:19). Following Jesus involves making a difference in the lives of other people so that they too become followers of Jesus. Just as Jesus was sent by the Father to do the Father's works in the world (John 5:36), Christians are sent by Jesus (John 20:21). The kingdom work of God extends beyond the borders of the church.

Jesus came to set people free from what binds them (Isa 61:1–3; Luke 4:17–21). When Jesus ministered in Galilee and Judea he forgave sins and freed people from sickness, poverty, grief, shame, and fear. He did not minister within the church but to the world, in order to draw the world into his church. The early church did this also. They took seriously the idea that they must minister to both the church and the world. The Emperor Julian in approximately 360 AD wrote regarding the Christians of his time, "For it is disgraceful when no Jew is a beggar and the impious Galileans [the name given by Julian to Christians] support our poor in addition to their own."[1] Christian ministry goes beyond the walls of the church and into the streets and the marketplace.

What then is the right paradigm for ministry? According to the New Testament, it is not the job of a few people to do the work on behalf of all.

1. Julian the apostate 'Letter to Arsacius'

It is the privilege of believers to be part of the body of Christ; each one is called to minister both inside and outside the church. Because of this, spiritual gifts are not used only by a paid few, or used only for a few minutes on Sunday morning, or even used only within the church. The Spirit gives gifts to all the people of God in order that the ministry to which we are called may be effectively carried out, both within the church and within the world.

3

Jesus and the Gifts of the Spirit

THE BIG DIFFERENCE BETWEEN the Old Testament and the New Testament is the coming of Jesus Christ. In the Old Testament, God spoke to people through prophets, "but in these last days he has spoken to us by his Son" (Heb 1:2). In the Gospel stories, God was physically present in Jesus. In other words, when Jesus spoke, God spoke. When Jesus acted, God acted. Therefore, Jesus is utterly central to what God has to say in the New Testament. (He is central to the Old Testament as well, but it is more veiled there).

Most Christians have no trouble agreeing that Jesus is God in the flesh. But the confession that Jesus is God can have an interesting and unhelpful result in the thinking of many Christians. Sometimes we forget that Jesus is actually also fully human. The early Christian creeds made sure to emphasize both the deity and the humanity of Jesus because both are vital to our salvation. The Chalcedon Creed (451), for example, declares: "We, then, following the holy Fathers, all with one consent, teach men to confess one and the same Son, our Lord Jesus Christ, the same perfect in Godhead and also *perfect in manhood*; truly God and *truly man, of reasonable soul and body*; consubstantial with the Father according to the Godhead, and *consubstantial with us according to the Manhood; in all things like unto us, without sin.*" Jesus cannot be Savior if he is not God, and he cannot be our representative and substitute if he is not human.

So we must remember, then, that Jesus is fully human. What does this mean for an understanding of spiritual gifts? If we think of Jesus as God only, then we will be inclined to think of Jesus doing miracles, healing the sick, teaching, prophesying, and knowing what people are thinking, only in terms of his deity. If Jesus did these things because he is divine, then how can any Christian do any of these things? After all, we are not God and cannot ever be God. However, if we think seriously about the humanity of Jesus, as portrayed in the Gospels, then there is a different way of understanding how Jesus did all these things. Luke's Gospel clearly portrays the humanity of Jesus. Jesus did not begin life knowing everything but rather as Luke tells us, "And Jesus *increased* in wisdom and in stature and in favor with God and man" (Luke 2:52).

Jesus did not do miracles or teach until he was baptized in the Jordan by John the Baptist (Luke 3:23). There he experienced the anointing of the Holy Spirit. "Now when all the people were baptized, and when Jesus also had been baptized and was praying, the heavens were opened, and the Holy Spirit descended on him in bodily form, like a dove" (Luke 3:21–22a). After his baptism and anointing by the Spirit, Jesus was led by the Spirit into the wilderness for forty days (Luke 4:1–2). "And Jesus returned in the power of the Spirit to Galilee" (Luke 4:14a). It was because of the anointing by the Holy Spirit that Jesus began his ministry and was enabled to carry it out. Jesus is truly God in the flesh, but he lived as a genuine human being, anointed by the Holy Spirit, in order to do the work of God. Jesus ministered in the power of the Holy Spirit.

Did Jesus exercise spiritual gifts? He must have, according to the paradigm I have just outlined. It has been said that Jesus exercised every spiritual gift listed in the New Testament, with the exception of speaking in tongues and interpretation of tongues. There is no record of Jesus speaking in tongues in the Gospels. It is not difficult, however, to find examples of Jesus speaking an utterance of wisdom, an utterance of knowledge, having faith, working miracles, speaking prophecy, and distinguishing between spirits—those gifts listed in 1 Cor 12:8–10. The gifts listed in Rom 12:6–8 are also evident in the life of Jesus—prophesying, serving, teaching, encouraging, contributing to the needs of others, leading, and showing mercy.

Emphasizing the humanity of Jesus provides a connection between the ministry of Jesus and the ministry of the church. The work of the church is in fact an extension of the work of Jesus, as the opening to the book of Acts tells us. "In the first book, O Theophilus, I have dealt with all that Jesus *began* to do and teach" (Acts 1:1). By God's grace we are given a share in the ministry of Jesus and can share in his power and authority. Jesus relied on the power of the Spirit to do the work of God. The church is similarly equipped to do the work of God because Jesus has given us his Spirit (Acts 2:33), who has given each believer spiritual gifts.

4

Spiritual Gifts and the Body of Christ

THE NEW TESTAMENT OFTEN describes the church as the body of Christ
(Rom 12:4–5; Eph 1:22–23; 2:14–16; 3:6; 4:4, 12–16; 5:23; Col 1:18, 24;
2:19; 3:15). The body metaphor means that each believer is connected to
Christ as head and connected to every other believer. This has implications
for an understanding of spiritual gifts.

The most well-known spiritual gifts chapter (1 Cor 12) explores what
it means to be the body of Christ. "For just as the body is one and has many
members, and all the members of the body, though many, are one body, so
it is with Christ. For in one Spirit we were all baptized into one body—Jews
or Greeks, slaves or free—and all were made to drink of one Spirit" (1 Cor
12:12–13). Paul emphasizes the unity of the body along with its diversity.
A body is not a collection of disparate parts without connection to one
another, but rather its many parts are integrally connected. Otherwise the
parts would not be a body at all. But since there is only one Holy Spirit
given by Jesus, we cannot be other than one body.

And the body is made up of diverse parts.

> For the body does not consist of one member but of many. If the
> foot should say, 'Because I am not a hand, I do not belong to the
> body,' that would not make it any less a part of the body. And if
> the ear should say, 'Because I am not an eye, I do not belong to
> the body,' that would not make it any less a part of the body. If
> the whole body were an eye, where would be the sense of hear-
> ing? If the whole body were an ear, where would be the sense of
> smell? But as it is, God arranged the members in the body, each
> one of them, as he chose. If all were a single member, where would

the body be? As it is, there are many parts, yet one body (1 Cor 12:14–20).

The diversity of the body parts results in a diversity of gifts in the body. But the gifts are given to be used by the one body. And the one body is to use the gifts according to the purposes of God and in the service of Jesus. "Now there are varieties of gifts, but the same Spirit; and there are varieties of service, but the same Lord; and there are varieties of activities, but it is the same God who empowers them all in everyone" (1 Cor 12:4–6). Notice the reference to the Trinity in these verses. The Holy Spirit distributes the gifts to whomever he wills (1 Cor 12:7). These are given to make possible the different kinds of service (ministry) in which the Lord Jesus would have us participate. And God (the Father) is at work in the people of God as they are equipped to minister like Jesus (see Phil 2:13; Heb 13:20–21).

Although Jesus exercised most of (or possibly all) the spiritual gifts listed in the New Testament, we should not expect that any one Christian would possess all the gifts. The work of God is no longer done by Jesus directly in the present but by his body, the church. The gifts are therefore distributed among every member of the body. Each person has gifts and is given corresponding ministries. But no person can lay claim to having all the gifts. Since no one individual in the body of Christ is equipped with every gift, this produces real interdependence. "If all were a single member, where would the body be? As it is, there are many parts, yet one body" (1 Cor 12:19-20). The human body shows us the necessity of interdependence. In the physical body, the eyes cannot function without blood vessels and the brain. The blood vessels are unable to do their job without the heart and the lungs. The feet do not work without the spinal column and the brain. I need not go on.

In the body of Christ it is not desirable for one person to act independently of others. God has not given us gifts for the benefit of ourselves as individuals but for the benefit of others. We are, therefore, all dependent on one another for our needs to be met. This is the will of God, not an accident. As a human being, Jesus depended on both his Father in heaven and on the Holy Spirit, in order to live his life and minister to others. He also depended on other humans to provide his physical needs. Dependence may not sit well with our individualistic culture, but it is the way the body of Christ must operate. Thus you cannot simply call upon the Holy Spirit to provide you with whatever gift you desire at the time. Instead, you need to rely on another person who has the desired gift to meet your needs. By the same token, you must use your gifts to meet the needs of others.

The church is the body of Christ. Consequently, we are each like a different body part. Every part of the body depends for its functioning and well-being on every other part. The gifts and ministries of each believer complement one another. Interdependence and not independence is a key aspect of being the church and thus vital in our use of spiritual gifts. This diversity-in-unity and unity-in-diversity is one way the triune God (Father, Son, and Holy Spirit), who is himself one and three simultaneously, shows forth his glory to the world.

5

Gifts, Grace, and Christian Maturity

THERE ARE A FEW more important aspects of spiritual gifts to discuss before going on to consider individual gifts. These aspects of spiritual gifts are diverse, making this chapter rather wide ranging in topics. It covers grace, faith, diversity of gifts, human involvement in receiving gifts, the outward focus of their use, the continuation of spiritual gifts in the present age, and the creative use of gifts for changing times.

The Greek word often translated as "spiritual gift" is *charisma*. This is very similar to another Greek word, *charis*, which means "grace." This would suggest a connection between spiritual gifts and grace. And indeed the two words appear together in Rom 12:6. "Having gifts [*charismata*— plural of *charisma*] that differ according to the grace [*charis*] given to us" (Rom 12:6a). We should remember the connection between the gifts and grace so that arrogance does not overtake us. The gifts a person is given are not determined by performance but by grace. Gifts are given without reference to merit; we do not receive them according to our own achievements. The Holy Spirit determines which gift to give to which person (1 Cor 12:11). Possibly you feel that you deserve something and someone else does not. Or possibly you believe the opposite, that you are unworthy to receive a certain gift. But this is not how grace operates. We must, therefore, not congratulate ourselves on the gifts we possess but see these as the gifts they are. Spiritual gifts are just that, gifts, given to us, not earned.

"For by the grace given to me I say to everyone among you not to think of himself more highly than he ought to think, but to think with sober judgment, each according to the measure of faith that God has assigned"

(Rom 12:3). Gifts must be used according to the faith given by God. Some have a greater measure of faith and some a lesser measure. Since this is determined by God, not by us, we cannot boast. Whatever the measure of faith, use your gifts accordingly. If you have been given little faith, then don't overstep that faith. If you have been given great faith, then use your gifts boldly.

There is a great diversity of gifts. Several are listed in Rom 12 and 1 Cor 12. The list includes prophecy, service, teaching, exhortation/encouragement, contributing, leading, showing mercy, utterance of wisdom, utterance of knowledge, faith, healing, working of miracles, distinguishing between spirits, speaking in tongues, interpretation of tongues, helping, and administration. Paul refers to marriage and singleness as gifts (1 Cor 7:7). It has been said that martyrdom is a gift (1 Cor 13:3). Two men were equipped by the Holy Spirit with the skills for working the ornate crafts required to build the tabernacle (Exod 31:1–5). It is thus possible that other gifts are available from the Holy Spirit that are not listed in either the Old Testament or the New. So we should restrict neither the generosity nor the creativity of the Spirit in regard to gifts.

Although there may be more gifts, the ones listed in the New Testament can generally be divided into two categories. "As each has received a gift, use it to serve one another, as good stewards of God's varied grace: whoever speaks, as one who speaks oracles of God; whoever serves, as one who serves by the strength that God supplies—in order that in everything God may be glorified through Jesus Christ. To him belong glory and dominion forever and ever. Amen" (1 Pet 4:10–11). There are speaking gifts and service gifts. Speaking gifts would include prophecy, teaching, exhortation/encouragement, utterance of wisdom, utterance of knowledge, speaking in tongues, and interpretation of tongues. Service gifts would include service, giving, leading, acts of mercy, healing, working of miracles, helping, and administration. Whichever gift and whichever category of gift, the goal is that in using these gifts for the sake of others God may be praised.

The gifts are distributed by the Holy Spirit, but this does not mean there is no human involvement in receiving them. Paul exhorts the Corinthians to eagerly desire spiritual gifts and indeed to desire the higher gifts, particularly prophecy (1 Cor 12:31; 14:1, 39). Therefore, it is appropriate to ask for them. Paul told Timothy, "Do not neglect the gift you have, which was given you by prophecy when the council of elders laid their hands on you" (1 Tim 4:14). Human action—the prayers and prophetic word of the elders—resulted in Timothy receiving a gift. Others may be able to impart a gift through the laying on of hands, and praying for others is always appropriate. Gifts can also grow in scope and effectiveness. Timothy was told "to fan into flame the gift of God" (2 Tim 1:6). Thus there is some action to be taken by us to see the gifts grow and mature. There is no good reason to be passive about spiritual gifts. The gifts can be sought after and prayed about. This is true of both those we desire and those we already possess.

Let us then seek out spiritual gifts, not for our own sake but for the sake of others. Eagerness for gifts must be tempered by a desire to build up the church (1 Cor 14:12). The purpose of gifts is not that the individual would appear to be spiritual, but that the church would be edified. "What then, brothers? When you come together, each one has a hymn, a lesson, a revelation, a tongue, or an interpretation. *Let all things be done for building up*" (1 Cor 14:26). Within the context of church life, the gifts function to meet the needs of others rather than the needs of the one who exercises the gift. We find a precedent for this practice within the life of the Trinity. Father, Son, and Holy Spirit do not exist for their own glory but give glory to one another (e.g., John 17:1). When our focus in exercising the gifts is outward and not inward, this develops interdependence in the community of faith.

Another implication of this outward focus is that ministry extends beyond the bounds of the church. The word "build up" (or "edify"), often used in 1 Cor 14, is closely connected to the word Jesus used when he declared, "And I tell you, you are Peter, and on this rock I will *build* my church, and the gates of hell shall not prevail against it" (Matt 16:18). The gifts of the Spirit are, therefore, intended to both *build* the church by bringing people into it, and *build up* the church by maturing and meeting the needs of those who are within it. The church need not be inwardly focused as a body, just as individual Christians should not be inwardly focused in their use of the gifts within church. Use your gifts for others in whatever sphere God has placed you.

Although there are claims to the contrary, the gifts continue to be distributed in the church by the Holy Spirit in the present. Certain kinds of Christians insist that spiritual gifts have ceased now that we have a complete Bible. One passage often cited in favor of their argument is 1 Cor 13:8–10— "Love never ends. As for prophecies, they will pass away; as for tongues, they will cease; as for knowledge, it will pass away. For we know in part and we prophesy in part, but when the perfect comes, the partial will pass away." According to this argument, what is perfect is the canon of Scripture. However, this interpretation has removed the verse completely out of its context, both the immediate context of the passage and the wider context of the book. The immediate context of the cessation of gifts is knowing and being known by God—"For now we see in a mirror dimly, but then face to face. Now I know in part; then I shall know fully, even as I have been fully known" (1 Cor 13:12). It is difficult to argue that we currently know God as fully as he knows us, even though we have the whole Bible. We will not know God fully until we see the face of Jesus when he returns for his people.

The wider context of the book suggests that "perfect" is connected to Christian maturity. The vocabulary used in 1 Cor 13:10—"but when the perfect [*telios*] comes, the partial will pass away [*katargeō*]"—is the same as the vocabulary used in 1 Cor 2:6—"Yet among the mature [*telios*] we do impart wisdom, although it is not a wisdom of this age or of the rulers of this age, who are doomed to pass away [*katargeō*]." This implies that the goal of the gifts of the Spirit is the maturity of the body of Christ. When the church has been completely built, by bringing in all those who are to be a part of the bride of Christ, and when that bride is built up to maturity, then there will be no more need for the gifts of the Spirit. When Jesus returns, the present needs of the body will no longer exist. No more sick will need to be healed, no more ignorant will need to be taught, no more sorrowing will need to be comforted, and no more destitute will need mercy. So the gifts will not be necessary. The gifts will cease to exist when the kingdom has come in its fullness and not before.

Before moving on to discuss the individual gifts, there is one final point to be made regarding the way gifts are connected to ministries. Each gift may be used for many different ministries. There are a great many needs in both the church and the world, and these require creative use of gifts to meet those needs. As Paul observed, "I have become all things to all people, that by all means I might save some" (1 Cor 9:22). So in using spiritual gifts to meet need, there is potential for creative change and growth. There is no reason why a person need continue to use a gift in only one ministry for life. The church can creatively operate the gifts in many different ministries as different needs arise and as different ways of meeting needs are required in the culture. Similarly, multiple gifts can be used together for the one minis- try. The different gifts may be present in the one person or in many people. The creativity of the Spirit in these matters need never be underestimated.

Therefore, use your gifts with humility and for the benefit of others. Aim to see people come into the church in accordance with God's grace, and strive to help other Christians mature in the faith. As long as there are needs in the church and the world, the Holy Spirit will continue to distribute gifts and Christians can continue to share in the ministry of Jesus. God will continue to work among his people in diverse ways until Jesus comes again.

Part 2

Individual Gifts

6

Prophecy

"Having gifts that differ according to the grace given to us, let us use them: *if prophecy, in proportion to our faith*" (Rom 12:6).

"to another the working of miracles, *to another prophecy*, to another the ability to distinguish between spirits, to another various kinds of tongues, to another the interpretation of tongues" (1 Cor 12:10).

THE APOSTLE PAUL CONSIDERED prophecy to be the most useful gift in the church (1 Cor 14:1). For this reason, prophecy has been placed first in the discussion of individual gifts. Because of the significance of prophecy, this chapter is longer than others and is followed by a further chapter on testing prophecy.

What is prophecy? The simplest answer is that prophecy involves hearing words directly from God and speaking those words to others. Some Old Testament prophets wrote down their prophecies and these have formed books of the Bible. Other Old Testament prophets are mainly found within the books of Samuel, Kings, and Chronicles. It is important to note that there is a difference between Old Testament prophets and New Testament prophets. In the Old Testament the authority of the prophet of God could not be countered. If a prophet spoke, then that word was expected to be obeyed. In the New Testament those who prophesy carry less authority. Scripture is now more authoritative than prophecy since the Scripture has been completed. However, prophecy is still a very important gift and should not be ignored. "Do not despise prophecies" (1 Thess 5:20).

To understand prophecy it is best to begin with the life of Jesus. In his life, Jesus fulfilled the law and the prophets (Matt 5:17). Matthew records many Old Testament prophecies that were fulfilled in the life of Jesus (Matt 1:22; 2:17; 3:3; 8:17; 12:17; 13:35 etc.), demonstrating that prophecy points us to Jesus. Jesus indirectly called himself a prophet. "Truly, I say to you, no prophet is acceptable in his hometown" (Luke 4:24; see also 13:33). Certainly the people thought that he was a prophet (Luke 24:19; John 4:19). The soldiers mocked Jesus as a prophet before they crucified him (Matt 26:68). Many others perceived that Jesus is a prophet (Luke 7:16; John 6:14; 7:40; 9:17). But Jesus was more than just a prophet. He is the one of whom Moses prophesied, "The LORD your God will raise up for you a prophet like me from among you, from your brothers—it is to him you shall listen" (Deut 18:15).

The Gospels record many prophecies Jesus uttered during his life. He prophesied his own death (Matt 16:21), the signs of the end of the age (Matt 24), his resurrection (Matt 20:19), the betrayal of Judas (John 13:21), Peter's denial (Matt 26:34), and his assumption into glory (Matt 26:64). However, there is a real sense in which every word and every action of Jesus is prophetic. A prophet speaks words from God, but Jesus does more than this. John's Gospel makes it clear that Jesus is not just one who speaks words from God. He is the eternal Word, who was in the beginning with God and is God (John 1:1). Jesus' actions and words were done with the authority of the Father (John 14:10). The things Jesus spoke did not originate with him; he only spoke what the Father gave to him. "Whoever does not love me does not keep my words. And the word that you hear is not mine but the Father's who sent me" (John 14:24). The whole life of Jesus, not merely his words, reveals God to humanity.

Prophecy must point in some way to Jesus Christ. This is true of the Old Testament prophecies and it is true of New Testament prophecy. The Holy Spirit, who enables prophecy, points us to Christ. Jesus himself said as much. "I still have many things to say to you, but you cannot bear them now. When the Spirit of truth comes, he will guide you into all the truth, for he will not speak on his own authority, but whatever he hears he will speak, and he will declare to you the things that are to come. He will glorify me, for he will take what is mine and declare it to you. All that the Father has is mine; therefore I said that he will take what is mine and declare it to you" (John 16:12–15).

When the Spirit was poured out on the church, the people of God prophesied. "When the day of Pentecost arrived, they were all together in one place. And suddenly there came from heaven a sound like a mighty rushing wind, and it filled the entire house where they were sitting. And divided tongues as of fire appeared to them and rested on each one of them. And they were all filled with the Holy Spirit and began to speak in other tongues as the Spirit gave them utterance" (Acts 2:1–4). When the crowd heard this phenomenon, they wanted to know what on earth was going on and the apostle Peter explained this in terms of prophecy. "And in the last days it shall be, God declares, that I will pour out my Spirit on all flesh, and your sons and your daughters shall prophesy, and your young men shall see visions, and your old men shall dream dreams; even on my male servants and female servants in those days I will pour out my Spirit, and they shall prophesy" (Acts 2:17–18). This prophetic activity pointed the crowd to Jesus, as Peter's sermon evidences. "Men of Israel, hear these words: Jesus of Nazareth, a man attested to you by God . . . " (Acts 2:22).

Apart from affirming that prophecy points us to Jesus Christ, the day of Pentecost tells us that since every believer receives the indwelling Holy Spirit, every believer is in some sense a prophet. All the people of God will prophesy because all the people of God are people of the Spirit. This is not to say that every believer has the gift of prophecy. But in the broadest sense, each believer receives from God through the Spirit and proclaims to the world that Jesus is Lord. This is prophecy in its most basic form. In this way, all true evangelism is prophetic. When we tell people about Jesus, we are proclaiming in a prophetic way the word of God.

The events of Pentecost also demonstrate that prophecy has a place outside the church in proclaiming Christ to the world. In the Old Testament, prophecy was often uttered to (or against) nations or rulers outside Israel (e.g., Jer 46–51). In a similar way in Acts, prophecy is uttered, not just inside the church but also to the unbelieving world. This functions as a way of telling people about the lordship of Jesus. For example, when Stephen was confronted by the Sanhedrin, he made a long speech about the history of Israel, which ended like this: "You stiff-necked people, uncircumcised in heart and ears, you always resist the Holy Spirit. As your fathers did, so do you. Which of the prophets did your fathers not persecute? And they killed those who announced beforehand the coming of the Righteous One, whom you have now betrayed and murdered, you who received the law as delivered by angels and did not keep it" (Acts 7:51–53). Like the prophets who preceded him, Stephen spoke the truth to the men of the Sanhedrin about their own hearts. And like the prophets who preceded him, he was hated because of it (Acts 7:54–58).

But the book of Acts also contains several examples of the use of prophecy within the church. "Now in these days prophets came down from Jerusalem to Antioch. And one of them named Agabus stood up and foretold by the Spirit that there would be a great famine over all the world (this took place in the days of Claudius). So the disciples determined, every one according to his ability, to send relief to the brothers living in Judea. And they did so, sending it to the elders by the hand of Barnabas and Saul" (Acts 11:27–30). This passage tells us a number of things about prophecy. First of all, there were people in the church who prophesied often enough that they had the designation "prophet." To be designated as prophet suggests a regular use of the gift of prophecy along with recognition by the church that the words spoken are truly from the Holy Spirit. Second, the prophecy Agabus uttered was for the sake of the church. Because of this prediction, the church was able to prepare a response to the famine. Because the ancient world did not have rapid communication and fast transport, the church needed time to organize relief and send someone with the money to Judea. The use of prophecy in this instance was directed at believers to build up the church. In this respect, it is different to Pentecost and to Stephen's speech to the Sanhedrin.

A number of other prophets are mentioned in Acts. In Antioch there were prophets and teachers (Acts 13:1). Quite likely they used the two gifts in concert with one another. Judas and Silas are called prophets; they "encouraged and strengthened the brothers with many words" (Acts 15:32). Philip had four virgin daughters who prophesied (Acts 21:9), and Agabus is mentioned again in Acts 21:10–11. Some of these prophets used their gifts within the church to encourage believers. But others used their gift of prophecy both inside and outside the church. Saul, otherwise known as Paul, is called a prophet in Acts 13:1. Much of what is recorded about Paul in Acts involves evangelism and church planting. Paul used his gifts for the purpose of building the church in number. However, the epistles suggest that he also used his gifts within the church. It is possible to do both.

Directions about the use of the gift of prophecy are concentrated in First Corinthians, but it is not the only book to instruct us about the gift.

The first epistle to mention prophecy is Romans. "Having gifts that differ according to the grace given to us, let us use them: if prophecy, in proportion to our faith" (Rom 12:6). There are limits placed on the ability to prophecy in accordance with the proportion of faith gifted to the individual. A similar warning is given in Rom 12:3. The person with the gift of prophecy does not have unlimited powers to predict the future or even to provide words of encouragement. But each person must exercise the gift as much as the allotment of faith given by God allows, and not presume to go beyond that. Prophecy can be tested, but there is always an element of subjectivity to the prophetic since it is not simply a matter of repeating Scripture. The prophet must have humility in speaking and also confidence to speak "as one who speaks oracles of God" (1 Pet 4:11a). Yet there is a self-applied boundary to prophecy, knowing that sometimes it is purely speculation about what God is saying. For this reason, the person who prophesies should spend much time in prayer and the Scripture in order to better discern the voice of the Holy Spirit.

Much of 1 Cor 14 is given over to a discussion of prophecy and tongues. (I will discuss speaking in tongues later.) The chapter contains important teaching about prophecy and instructions about its appropriate use.

> Pursue love, and earnestly desire the spiritual gifts, especially that you may prophesy. For one who speaks in a tongue speaks not to men but to God; for no one understands him, but he utters mysteries in the Spirit. On the other hand, the one who prophesies speaks to people for their upbuilding and encouragement and consolation. The one who speaks in a tongue builds up himself, but the one who prophesies builds up the church. Now I want you all to speak in tongues, but even more to prophesy. The one who prophesies is greater than the one who speaks in tongues, unless someone interprets, so that the church may be built up. Now, brothers, if I come to you speaking in tongues, how will I benefit you unless I bring you some revelation or knowledge or prophecy or teaching? (1 Cor 14:1–6).

First, it must be noted that this chapter follows on from what is often called the "love chapter." All the gifts of the Spirit must be used in love. However, it is false to suggest that we are to pursue love *instead* of the gifts. The whole Christian life is lived in love. Spiritual gifts are not in opposition to love. Rather the gifts the Spirit bestows on the church are the practical tools by which love can be exercised effectively within the body. They cannot be appropriately exercised without love, but love is not practically exercised without any capacity to act. We are enabled to act by the Spirit, who gives us gifts by which to minister to one another and to the world in love. Therefore, Paul insists in 1 Cor 14:1 that Christians are to both "pursue love, *and* earnestly desire the spiritual gifts."

The gift most to be desired, according to 1 Cor 14:1, is prophecy. The reason this gift is so emphasized in the passage has to do with the contrast between prophecy and tongues. The Corinthian church was apparently very keen on appearing spiritual. The word that is translated in 1 Cor 14:1 and 1 Cor 12:1 as "spiritual gifts" (*pneumatikos*) is a different word to the one that is used in other parts of these chapters (*charisma*). It can simply be translated as "spiritual." Possibly the Corinthians thought that speaking in tongues a lot made them appear spiritual. Earlier in the letter Paul told them that they were in fact not spiritual people but infants in Christ (1 Cor 3:1) since they were bickering with one another and divided (1 Cor 3:2–4). Therefore, he insists that the mark of spirituality is not speaking in tongues but submission to Jesus Christ as Lord. "Now concerning spiritual gifts (*pneumatikos*), brothers, I do not want you to be uninformed. You know that when you were pagans you were led astray to mute idols, however you were led. Therefore I want you to understand that no one speaking in the Spirit of God ever says 'Jesus is accursed!' and no one can say 'Jesus is Lord' except in the Holy Spirit" (1 Cor 12:1–3). The gift of prophecy is not a mark of spirituality either since it is a gift not an achievement. If it is exercised without love then it is not helpful (1 Cor 13:2). But prophecy is more directly valuable to the church than speaking in tongues since a tongue is unintelligible to the speaker and the hearers. But prophecy is understandable to both and therefore edifies the church. For this reason, we are told to eagerly desire the gift of prophecy.

Prophecy is a valuable gift within the church, but it must not be used indiscriminately. "Let two or three prophets speak, and let the others weigh what is said. If a revelation is made to another sitting there, let the first be silent. For you can all prophesy one by one, so that all may learn and all be encouraged, and the spirits of prophets are subject to prophets. For God is not a God of confusion but of peace. As in all the churches of the saints" (1 Cor 14:29–33). The gifts must be used in an orderly way. Many people in one church may have the gift of prophecy and each can use that gift in turn. When every person is allowed to speak what they are given to say by the Holy Spirit, then the church can be instructed and encouraged.

The statement "The spirits of prophets are subject to prophets" (1 Cor 14:32) may be understood in two ways. First, it implies there is no compulsion from the Holy Spirit in prophecy, no automatic speech, so the person who prophesies actually has control of what comes out of the mouth. The prophet may choose to speak the prophecy or hold off until later. Second, it suggests that prophets may sometimes mix the thoughts of their own spirits with the words that come from the Holy Spirit. The maturity of the prophet comes into play here. The person prophesying may not have had sufficient experience of listening to the Holy Spirit and thus may get the message distorted. For these reasons, it is necessary to weigh what is said. Other prophets are in the best place to evaluate prophetic words, but the whole church is responsible for this task since the words are addressed to the whole church. (There is more about testing prophecy in the next chapter.)

The two passages (1 Cor 14:1–6 and 1 Cor 14:29–33) together provide the parameters of prophecy. Its use is for instruction, encouragement (1 Cor 14:31), unbuilding, and consolation (1 Cor 14:3). Lest we think this implies that prophecies can only ever be positive and happy-sounding, we must consider what these words actually mean. Let's begin with the word "instruction" or "learning." What would a prophecy help people to learn? The learning may involve some doctrine (2 Tim 3:14), but most of the references to learning in the New Testament involve, not intellectual learning, but learning to do something. "What you have learned and received and heard and seen in me—*practice these things*, and the God of peace will be with you" (Phil 4:9). Christians need to learn to put their religion into practice by caring for family (1 Tim 5:4), instead of learning to be idle (1 Tim 5:13), and learn to devote themselves to doing good (Tit 3:14). This flows out of learning Christ (Eph 4:20). Jesus wants us to learn from him (Matt 11:29). Jesus himself learned obedience (Heb 5:8). Teaching can provide instruction in doctrine, which is valuable. But the value of the prophetic word is that it helps people to apply teaching in practical situations in their lives. Learning from a prophetic word overflows into obedience, mercy, discipleship, and practical love. This may involve rebuke to help the church learn what they are failing to do.

"Encouragement" can have several nuances, including: appeal to, urge, exhort, encourage, request, implore, and entreat. This will be explored more fully later (in the chapter on the gift of exhortation/encouragement), but for now it can be said that, while this is mostly positive, it can involve exhorting people to do what is right. It is not to be associated with "fluffy" inspirational sayings. Prophecy is for edification. It builds us up morally and spiritually. It may also provide comfort (1 Cor 14:3). Prophecy can be meaty and strong even as it is comforting. It does not need to be "sweet" and "happy." The people of God can be edified and comforted by strong words from God.

Prophecy is not primarily a matter of predicting some future event. It may involve prediction (Acts 11:28), but more often involves application of the Scriptures to a situation facing the church. Teaching expounds the Bible, but prophecy applies teaching to a situation in the church or the life of an individual. Sometimes prophecy will provide direction to a person who has need of it. An example of this type of prophecy is found in Acts 13:2—"While they were worshiping the Lord and fasting, the Holy Spirit said, 'Set apart for me Barnabas and Saul for the work to which I have called them.'" Prophecy can enable the church to put its emphasis in the right place or to open up new ways of thinking. It can provide gifts and start people in new ministries (1 Tim 4:14). The church is impoverished without prophecy since without this gift we are left to our own reason and feelings about what to do. Through prophecy, direct words from God can flow into the church, enabling discipleship, bringing more effectiveness in ministry, and encouraging deeper relationship with Father, Son, and Spirit.

Prophecy has a clear place within the church, but spiritual gifts are also given to bring new people into the church. So prophecy has a place outside the church. I have already mentioned the events of Pentecost when the believers spoke prophetically in foreign tongues and proclaimed the gospel to the people from other nations. But there are other examples in the New Testament of prophecy being directed to those outside the church. Paul explains how prophecy impacts unbelievers.

> Thus tongues are a sign not for believers but for unbelievers, while prophecy is a sign not for unbelievers but for believers. If, therefore, the whole church comes together and all speak in tongues, and outsiders or unbelievers enter, will they not say that you are out of your minds? But if all prophesy, and an unbeliever or outsider enters, he is convicted by all, he is called to account by all, the secrets of his heart are disclosed, and so, falling on his face, he will worship God and declare that God is really among you (1 Cor 14:22–25).

Prophecy will bring conviction of sin to the unbeliever because the prophetic word will lay open the secrets of the heart. Bringing conviction of sin is the work of the Holy Spirit. "And when he [the Helper] comes, he will convict the world concerning sin and righteousness and judgment" (John 16:8). The world does not recognize Jesus (John 1:10), even though Jesus was sent into the world to save it (John 3:17). The world hates Jesus (John 7:7) and is judged (John 12:31). Since the world does not believe in Jesus, the Holy Spirit convicts them of sin (John 16:9). The operation of the prophetic gift is one way in which the Holy Spirit moves in the world, that is, towards those outside the church, to bring about that conviction of sin.

Another example of prophecy directed to those outside the church is found in Rev 11. The book of Revelation is itself a prophecy addressed to the church (Rev 1:3). Among those who have been slain for the name of Jesus are the prophets (Rev 18:4). But Rev 11 mentions two prophets specifically, who prophecy for 1,260 days while the holy city is trampled by Gentiles (vv. 2–3). They are very powerful, performing miracles and sending plagues and judgments on the earth (vv. 4–6). However, the beast overpowers them and they die. Their bodies lie in the streets of Jerusalem and the people of the earth rejoice over their deaths (vv. 7–10). After three and a half days, they are raised from the dead and taken up to heaven (vv. 11–12). Of course, Revelation is full of symbols and cannot be understood in a literal way. But what is clear in this account is that those who prophesy do so, not to the church but to the wicked people who live on the earth and are opposed to Jesus. They testify to Jesus and are killed for it. So although prophecy is given to those outside the church, this does not always bring people into the church.

Jesus was a great prophet; his entire life, not just his words, speaks to us about God. Prophecy is a very important gift and one that should be sought because it benefits the body of Christ greatly. Words from God come through the prophet to the church. These words apply the Scripture to a particular situation. Prophecy serves to build up believers if used appropriately. It is sometimes predictive but mainly encourages and exhorts believers. It can serve as a means to convict sinners of the truth about Jesus. Because it is such a powerful gift it needs to be used wisely and tested carefully by the church. For this reason, I have devoted the next chapter to discussing how to test prophecy.

7

Testing Prophecy

PROPHECIES NEED TO BE tested. "Do not quench the Spirit. Do not despise prophecies, but test everything; hold fast what is good" (1 Thess 5:19–21). One of the reasons why prophecy is not encouraged in the church is because of fear; what if someone says something weird or outrageous or heretical? Careful testing of prophecy is the remedy for these fears. Since the Bible is clear that we should not prevent the Holy Spirit speaking, it is important that a proper procedure be followed in order to know whether the Spirit is truly speaking.

Foundational to testing prophecy is the truth that "the testimony of Jesus is the spirit of prophecy" (Rev 19:10). The Holy Spirit does not speak on his own but tells us about Jesus (John 16:12–15). We should, therefore, be wary of prophecy that does not in some way speak about Jesus, his person, his work, his will, or his love for us. It does not need to repeat the Bible in rote fashion since there is a broad range of topics that may be considered to be about Jesus. But prophecy must point us to Jesus. The church must discern whether the prophetic word glorifies Jesus or whether it gives glory or attention elsewhere.

Some further tests applicable to prophecy are found in 1 John 4. There John writes, "Beloved, do not believe every spirit, but test the spirits to see whether they are from God, for many false prophets have gone out into the world" (1 John 4:1). What follows are several ways of testing the spirits.

John's first test concerns a genuinely human Jesus. "By this you know the Spirit of God: every spirit that confesses that Jesus Christ has come in the flesh is from God, and every spirit that does not confess Jesus is not from God. This is the spirit of the antichrist, which you heard was coming and now is in the world already" (1 John 4:2–3). Jesus did not come merely to give us some sayings like the Sermon on the Mount and the Lord's Prayer. He could have posted us a letter for that. No, he came into the world as a flesh and blood human being, who lived a human life and experienced all the things human beings experience: birth, childhood, hunger, thirst, cold, heat, weariness, loneliness, friendship, betrayal, and finally ignoble death. The Spirit will not convey a picture of an unreal Jesus, because a false Jesus cannot help us, comfort us, or strengthen us. If what is said is not consistent with a fully human Jesus, then the prophecy is false.

The second test concerns the community of the church, beginning with the apostles. "They are from the world; therefore they speak from the world, and the world listens to them. We are from God. Whoever knows God listens to us; whoever is not from God does not listen to us. By this we know the Spirit of truth and the spirit of error" (1 John 4:5–6). According to this test, the one who speaks the truth listens to "us." Who is the "us" to whom John refers? There are two sets of people to whom we must listen. The first are the apostles of Christ; their testimony is recorded in the Bible. This is a way of saying that any prophecy must conform to what the Bible says. God is not divided; the Holy Spirit will not contradict what God has said in his word. The second set of people John is referring to is the church. Prophets need to listen to the church just as much as the church needs to listen to prophets. We are not individuals who can speak without reference to one another. We are the body of Christ and individually members of that body (1 Cor 1:27). We need to submit to one another (Eph 5:21) and honor one another (Rom 12:10). In effect, we must honor one another by speaking the truth in love (Eph 4:15), including correcting what is an incorrect understanding of God given in a prophecy. Both giving and receiving correction is difficult and it must be done in love for the sake of the other.

This brings me to the third test.

> Beloved, let us love one another, for love is from God, and whoever loves has been born of God and knows God. Anyone who does not love does not know God, because God is love. In this the love of God was made manifest among us, that God sent his only Son into the world, so that we might live through him. In this is love, not that we have loved God but that he loved us and sent his Son to be the propitiation for our sins. Beloved, if God so loved us, we also ought to love one another (1 John 4:7–11).

This test hinges on love. God is love, so no matter how amazing and profound the prophecy, it is not valid if it is not given in love. Arrogance has no place in the prophetic word. In order to be an instrument of God to the church, we must die to our own will and pride and submit ourselves to the love of God. Then we can be a channel of that love to others. Correction must be done in love. Words also need to be received in love (see 1 Pet 4:8). Prophecy will not always be given in a way that is pleasing. Sometimes it offends our sensibilities or is awkward or clumsy. But love will overlook these things. The important thing is to consider the other person when speaking or receiving prophecy.

The fourth test is also about love. "No one has ever seen God; if we love one another, God abides in us and his love is perfected in us. By this we know that we abide in him and he in us, because he has given us of his Spirit" (1 John 4:12–13). To understand this better we must consider another passage. "And it is my prayer that your love may abound more and more, with knowledge and all discernment, so that you may *approve* what is excellent, and so be pure and blameless for the day of Christ, filled with the fruit of righteousness that comes through Jesus Christ, to the glory and praise of God" (Phil 1:9–11). In Phil 1:10, the ESV uses the word "approve," but the Greek word is the same as the word "test" in 1 John 4:1—"*test* the spirits." The way to test what is good is to have love that abounds in knowledge and discernment. Thus having knowledge and discernment is part of God's love being made complete in us. Love is not a feeling but something powerful, able to understand what is good and to produce in us holiness and righteousness. This kind of love is not automatic in the Christian life. We must seek it and pray for it because this love will enable us to hear the Spirit's voice clearly.

Test five considers whether the prophecy exalts Jesus as Savior. "And we have seen and testify that the Father has sent his Son to be the Savior of the world. Whoever confesses that Jesus is the Son of God, God abides in him, and he in God" (1 John 4:14–15). Prophecy testifies that Jesus is the Savior of the world. If it is a true prophecy then it will be centered on Jesus: his character, his glory, and what he has done for his people. This seems an obvious thing to say, but it bears repeating. When the focus of the church is on something or someone other than Jesus, then we know that we are no longer in the will of God and we are ineffective in the kingdom of God.

Jesus is the Savior of the *world*. His influence is not merely over the church and certainly not just over a small group of people. Often, then, prophecy may apply to a wider sphere than just the people who are present in a local church on Sunday morning. The Spirit may give a prophecy about the people Christians come in contact with in family life, in work, in day to day events like shopping or buying petrol. Prophecy may also have something to say about wider spheres, like the nation we live in, politics, economics, medicine, other nations, missions, or other wider concerns. Jesus Christ is the one who fills all things (Eph 4:10).

The sixth test again involves love. "So we have come to know and to believe the love that God has for us. God is love, and whoever abides in love abides in God, and God abides in him. By this is love perfected with us, so that we may have confidence for the day of judgment, because as he is so also are we in this world. There is no fear in love, but perfect love casts out fear. For fear has to do with punishment, and whoever fears has not been perfected in love" (1 John 4:16–18). There is no condemnation in Christ (Rom 8:1); a prophetic word should be encouraging (1 Cor 14:3). A word that condemns is not from the Holy Spirit. There is a difference between condemnation and exhortation. Condemnation puts a burden on the people of God to do what they cannot rightly do, but exhortation encourages them to live according to God's word. Exhortation can certainly challenge the ideas we hold dear and challenge the way we act, but it should not bring fear of punishment. "We may have confidence for the day of judgment" while we are "in Christ" because in him we have been judged and given God's favorable verdict. Believers have the righteousness of Christ (Phil 3:9). Therefore, nothing the Spirit speaks will suggest that God is angry with us or that he will abandon us.

Last of all, I suggest another test. This is not a test of the words spoken but of the character of the prophet. Paul told the Corinthian church: "And with them we are sending our brother whom we have often tested and found earnest in many matters, but who is now more earnest than ever because of his great confidence in you" (2 Cor 8:22). This speaks of a person who wants to serve in the church, but I believe we can apply a similar principle to prophets. Time is a good test of a prophet's character; over time the kind of person you are becomes evident to others. If a person is not of godly character, then we need to take care to scrutinize his or her words very carefully. I am hesitant to believe a word spoken by someone who has not demonstrated over time his or her willingness to listen to God and to obey God's commands.

Prophecy is such an important gift for the church that it must be used regularly in every congregation. Yet we cannot rely on emotional or subjective decisions regarding its accuracy. It must be tested carefully. However a prophecy is worded, the main issue is whether it is centered on glorifying Jesus and spoken in love. Both individual prophets and the church as a whole must learn to discern so that we might be led by Jesus, exalt him, and carefully obey his word to us.

8

Service

"Having gifts that differ according to the grace given to us,
let us use them . . . *if service, in our serving*" (Rom 12:6a, 7a).

THE GIFT OF SERVICE is evidenced by acts of service. It is a gift exercised through giving of the gifted person to others. Service is very practical in its outworking. Although it appears to have no "supernatural" overtones, it is nonetheless vital to the proclamation of the gospel and the proper functioning of the church.

Some people are more enabled for service than others are. In a sense, it seems odd that service is a gift since surely service is required of all believers. Yet a number of the gifts involve things all believers are expected to do. There is a sense in which all believers are prophets since each one can proclaim what God says. Each one is expected to give financially to the work of the kingdom. Everyone should show mercy. All Christians have faith. Yet these are listed as gifts of the Spirit in either Rom 12 or 1 Cor 12. There is a difference between the ordinary Christian life and those who have been extraordinarily gifted by the Holy Spirit in particular ways. So although all Christians must live lives of service to God and to others, it is plain that some Christians are given gifts to enable them to excel in this area.

As with the other gifts, we must begin with the life of Jesus. Jesus clearly exercised the gift of service. "The Son of Man came not to be served but to serve, and to give his life as a ransom for many" (Matt 20:28). Just as Jesus' service was to give his life up for others, the gift of service involves self-giving for the sake of others. Whatever service is rendered to the body of Christ, it will involve some cost to the person who serves. The cost may be time, energy, or money, but there will always be a cost. Although it may not involve laying down your life in such a complete way as Jesus did, it does require that those who serve put the needs of others before their own.

The Gospels record that the disciples served Jesus. One of Jesus' earliest miracles was healing Peter's mother-in-law. "He touched her hand, and the fever left her, and she rose and *began to serve him*" (Matt 8:15). Service was a response to what Jesus did for her. Other disciples also served Jesus. Several women served Jesus by providing for his needs (Luke 8:3) and some served him as he was dying (Matt 27:55). When Christians minister to the poor, the hungry, the naked, the sick, and those in prison, they are serving Jesus (Matt 25:31–46). Service to Jesus is a response to who he is and what he has done. Believers serve Jesus because he first came to serve us.

The book of Acts gives us further insight into the gift of service. In Acts 6:1–6, seven men were chosen to administer daily food distribution to widows in the church. This appointment enabled the apostles to be free to preach the word of God and to pray (vv. 2, 4). Those who were chosen to serve the Jerusalem church were "full of the Spirit and of wisdom" (v. 3). The task they performed was not trivial; it required a spiritual gift. Although the word *charisma* is not mentioned here, they needed the fullness and equipping of the Holy Spirit to do the task. The result of the service of the seven was that "the word of God continued to increase, and the number of the disciples multiplied greatly in Jerusalem, and a great many priests became obedient to the faith" (Acts 6:7). When those who served did what they were called to do, the apostles were able to do the task given to them—preach the word of God and pray. The body of Christ worked together in order to build the church in number. When gifts are used appropriately, then God's work is done. The gifts are not competitive but cooperative.

Just as the Jerusalem apostles needed people to serve so that they could get on with the task given them, Paul too needed people to minister to his needs while he was preaching the gospel. His missionary work took him all over the known world and was an intense task. Those who served Paul included Timothy and Erastus, who are mentioned by name in Acts 19:22. Paul also desired the service of Onesimus, slave of Philemon, since Paul was at that time in prison (Phlm 1:13). He commended Onesiphorus, who served Paul greatly in Ephesus (2 Tim 1:16–18). Service may involve meeting the needs of people who are particularly called to proclaim the gospel—missionaries, pastors, and evangelists—and Christians who are in prison for the faith, as are many in the persecuted church.

The people of God in general are also served (Rom 15:25). Service to the saints involves the proclamation of the gospel (2 Cor 3:3), and can include other things done to benefit the people of God (Heb 6:10). Even the Old Testament prophets served the saints by hearing and writing down words from God (1 Pet 1:12). In a sense, every gift of the Spirit is to be used to serve the people of God (1 Pet 4:10–11). Service to God's people can incorporate financial and practical actions. A prophet in Acts 11:28 predicted a severe famine over the Roman world and the Christians sent help to those in Judea. This famine was the reason that Paul was collecting for the Jerusalem church, as he describes in 2 Cor 8 and 9. This financial help was a service to the Lord's people (2 Cor 8:4; 9:1, 12–13). Service to the people of God has many possible forms: proclaiming the gospel, teaching the word of God, financial giving, or practical service, such as meeting the needs of others.

The apostles served the church by proclaiming the gospel. They were appointed to the ministry (service) of reconciliation (2 Cor 5:18), a ministry that comes from the Spirit. The ministry of the Spirit is a ministry of righteousness and it is glorious (2 Cor 3:7–9). Paul served the Gentiles and the other apostles served the Jews, but both served with the gospel. Effectively, then, service cannot be disconnected from the gospel. Whatever practical aspects service may include—meeting people's needs, financial giving, helping those who are preaching the gospel, proclaiming the gospel itself, helping the saints, administering the church's distribution of food— all service is centered on the gospel. We must not miss the connection between the gifts, in this case service, and the gospel of Christ. The gifts are not given apart from Christ; we serve Jesus first and one another second.

Can the gift of service (otherwise translated as ministry) be used outside of the church? Jesus laid down his life (Matt 20:28) so that all who are outside the church can become part of it. Paul speaks about his ministry (service) to the Gentiles (Rom 11:13; Gal 2:8). The Gentiles were far from God and brought near by the blood of Christ. So service to those outside the church is intended to bring them into the church. Christians serve people who are not part of the church in many ways. This involves meeting people's needs in the name of Jesus. Christians serve people outside the church by feeding the hungry, being Christians in politics, running playgroups, helping an elderly neighbor, or caring for the helpless. But it is always God's desire that the gifts of the Spirit produce fruit. The intention is to build the church, in this case by bringing people into the church.

Service seems to be an umbrella term that could encompass every gift and its use. All believers are servants of Jesus, of God, and of the gospel. We serve since Jesus served before us and we serve with him. Whatever gift we may be using should be used in service of others. But there are some who are clearly given the gift of service and therefore serve more consistently than others do. These people free up others to use their own gifts, particularly those who proclaim the gospel in words. By meeting people's practical needs, service shows people Jesus.

9

Teaching

"Having gifts that differ according to the grace given to us,
let us use them . . . *the one who teaches, in his teaching;*"
(Rom 12:6a, 7b).

THE GIFT OF TEACHING holds a very significant place in the life of the church. Being among the intelligible speech gifts it is of great benefit to believers. It gives content to the Christian faith.

Jesus taught a lot. He did this in many different settings: in synagogues (Matt 4:23; 13:54); beside the sea (Mark 2:13; 4:1); on a mountain (Matt 5:1–2); in the villages (Mark 6:6); in the cities (Matt 11:1); and in the temple (Mark 12:35). He taught both his disciples and the crowds (Matt 11:1; Mark 4:1). Wherever he went he taught people; teaching was quite central to the mission of Jesus. His teaching was with authority and that authority was clearly recognized by those who heard him (Matt 7:29). His teaching was motivated by compassion. "When he went ashore he saw a great crowd, and he had compassion on them, because they were like sheep without a shepherd. And he began to teach them many things" (Mark 6:34). People need the teaching of Jesus because without it they are like helpless sheep, wandering around with no direction, no protection, and no purpose. The teaching of Jesus communicates what people need to hear in order to have life.

But Jesus' teaching frequently divided people. He often taught in parables (Mark 4:2), and therefore his teaching separated people into those who understood and those who did not—"He who has ears to hear, let him hear" (Mark 4:9). Jesus' teaching provoked a response from people, often antagonistic. "And he was teaching them and saying to them, 'Is it not written, "My house shall be called a house of prayer for all the nations"? But you have made it a den of robbers.' And the chief priests and the scribes heard it and were seeking a way to destroy him, for they feared him, because all the crowd was astonished at his teaching" (Mark 11:17–18). "So Jesus proclaimed, as he taught in the temple, 'You know me, and you know where I come from . . . ' So they were seeking to arrest him . . . " (John 7:28–30 abridged). Teaching, then, cannot be neutral. It provokes a response from people and divides them into followers of Jesus or those who are opposed to Jesus.

Jesus taught about the kingdom of God (Matt 4:23). To his disciples only, Jesus taught that he would suffer and die and then be raised from the dead (Mark 8:31). He taught about the purpose of the temple—it is to be a house of prayer for all nations (Mark 11:17). He corrected the wrong teaching of the scribes (Mark 12:35). He taught about himself and the Father (John 7:28). What he taught came from the Father and had the authority of the Father (John 8:28). Since Jesus has gone back to the Father, he now sends the Holy Spirit to teach us (John 14:26). Christians are given the commission to make disciples and to teach them all that Jesus commanded (Matt 28:20). What Jesus taught must still be taught. We cannot rightly teach in our own authority or about ourselves but only about Jesus, the Father, and the kingdom of God, in the authority given by God in the gospel.

Jesus has not ceased to teach. The Book of Acts begins, "In the first book, O Theophilus, I have dealt with all that Jesus *began* to do and teach" (Acts 1:1). The teaching of the apostles in Acts continued the teaching Jesus began in the Gospels. However, the content of that teaching shifted slightly. The apostles taught about Jesus and his resurrection from the dead (Acts 4:2). Although Jesus taught that he would be raised from the dead, he only taught this to his disciples (Matt 16:21; 17:9, 23; 20:19; 26:32). But in Acts, the apostles proclaimed the resurrection of Jesus and taught it to every person within hearing (Acts 2:24, 32; 4:2, 10, 33).

Teaching is not always used within the church. In Acts, most people who were taught were not part of the church, although they often became part of the church by hearing the teaching about Jesus. In fact, the apostles taught the crowds in Jerusalem regularly. "And when they heard this, they entered the temple at daybreak and began to teach" (Acts 5:21a). "And every day, in the temple and from house to house, they did not cease teaching and preaching that the Christ is Jesus" (Acts 5:42). Barnabas and Paul taught the proconsul of Cyprus about the Lord Jesus (Acts 13:7, 12). Paul also taught philosophers in the Areopagus in Athens (Acts 17:19). The fact that the apostles taught the people in this way suggests that the line between evangelism and teaching is not solid. Teaching can help unbelievers become believers just as evangelism can. The weakness of much contemporary evangelism is its lack of content about Jesus. Since the apostles taught about Jesus to the crowds, who were as yet not part of the church, it is fruitful to teach unbelievers about Jesus, instead of merely giving a testimony or an invitation to church.

Teaching can also take place within the church. "And they devoted themselves to the apostles' teaching and the fellowship, to the breaking of bread and the prayers" (Acts 2:42). "For a whole year they [Barnabas and Saul] met with the church and taught a great many people" (Acts 11:26b). Paul and Barnabas also taught the church in Antioch for a year (Acts 5:35). Paul taught for a year and a half in Corinth (Acts 18:11). The time spent teaching the church was considerable. Presumably there was a lot to teach about Jesus and the Christian life. In his farewell speech to the Ephesian elders, Paul declared that he had taught them everything which is profitable (Acts 20:20). The last verse of Acts leaves Paul "proclaiming the kingdom of God and teaching about the Lord Jesus Christ with all boldness and without hindrance" (Acts 28:31). This emphasizes the most significant topics of teaching—the kingdom of God and the Lord Jesus Christ.

To us it is not surprising that teaching would take place within the church; this is what we expect. But it does not necessarily take place within a church building on a Sunday. The apostles taught in public and from house to house (Acts 20:20). Teaching went on while Paul was under house arrest (Acts 28:31). It often occurred in the synagogue if believers were there. It was not confined to a twenty-minute sermon on Sunday. In one instance, Paul talked all night and until daylight because he was leaving the next day (Acts 20:7–12).

Teaching is a very important gift, which is mentioned many times in the epistles. "And God has appointed in the church first apostles, second prophets, third teachers, then miracles, then gifts of healing, helping, administrating, and various kinds of tongues" (1 Cor 12:28). "And he gave the apostles, the prophets, the evangelists, the shepherds and teachers" (Eph 4:11). Teaching is given a prominent place among the gifts of the Spirit because it equips the body of Christ (Eph 4:12). Teaching is intended to help Christians come to maturity in Christ (Col 1:28). When the body of Christ is faithfully taught the truth, then Christians learn and grow and serve God effectively. Teachers have a responsibility to teach faithfully and carefully all that God has said (Acts 20:27; 2 Tim 2:15). As such, teachers will be judged more strictly than others will (Jas 3:1), and must therefore be careful that their teaching does not lead people astray. By the same token, those who are not teachers cannot blame the teachers if the hearer fails to discern what is true or false. John reminds us, "But the anointing that you received from him abides in you, and you have no need that anyone should teach you. But as his anointing teaches you about everything, and is true, and is no lie—just as it has taught you, abide in him" (1 John 2:27). The Holy Spirit abides in each believer and if we listen carefully to him, then we can discern truth or error in teaching.

Discerning truth or error is important since there are also false teachers active within the church. Some taught that circumcision was necessary for salvation (Acts 15:1; Gal 2:12). Other false teaching mentioned in the New Testament includes those who taught people to eat food sacrificed to idols and to practice sexual immorality (Rev 2:14, 20). Some taught Jewish myths (Titus 1:13–14). Others taught doctrines of demons, in particular that marriage must be avoided and certain foods should not be eaten (1 Tim 4:1–3). False teaching leads people away from following Jesus, away from godly behavior, and away from grace. It is to be avoided at all costs because it stunts maturity in the body of Christ and results in confusion. False teachers do not place Jesus and his work in the center of their teaching. They are always concerned to either add to or subtract from the message about Jesus.

The content of true teaching is Christ. Paul taught the way to life in Christ (1 Cor 4:17). The truth is in Jesus Christ and leads us to put off the old self and put on the new (Eph 4:21–24). The mystery of Christ is glorious and he is proclaimed and taught in order to perfect the people of God (Col 1:28). All Christians must teach one another by speaking the word of God in conversation (Col 3:16). Godliness and sound doctrine should be taught (1 Tim 4:7–11). Teaching includes instruction about how to live with others in loving and respectful ways (1 Tim 6:2). Teaching is often about practical ways of living, such as how to live reverent lives, how to have self control, and to love husbands and children (Titus 2:1–6). The way to discern if teaching is true is to ask whether Jesus is glorified by it. If Jesus and his work are sidelined, then the teaching is false. If what is taught leads to ungodly behavior or encourages people away from holiness, then it is false. Teaching is always about the content of the gospel.

Teachers, and indeed all Christians, must grow in their understanding of the word of God. In Acts, Apollos was teaching about Jesus from his limited knowledge, so he was instructed in order to do this better (Acts 18:25). The writer to the Hebrews told the church, "For though by this time you ought to be teachers, you need someone to teach you again the basic principles of the oracles of God. You need milk, not solid food" (Heb 5:12). It is not only the responsibility of teachers to teach the church, but it is the responsibility of all Christians to learn so that they can teach others. "Let the word of Christ dwell in you richly, teaching and admonishing one another in all wisdom, singing psalms and hymns and spiritual songs, with thankfulness in your hearts to God" (Col 3:16).

The final topic is the subject of great debate in churches, that is, whether it is acceptable for women to teach. The verse on which the argument hinges is 1 Tim 2:12—"I do not permit a woman to teach or to exercise authority over a man; rather, she is to remain quiet." This is often used along with 1 Cor 14:35—"If there is anything they desire to learn, let them ask their husbands at home. For it is shameful for a woman to speak in church." The argument is that if a woman is able to teach men, then this will disrupt the order of the family, which has been established in creation. This argument ignores the evidence of the New Testament, which frees women to be more than just wives and mothers. The Holy Spirit is given to both men and women. The gifts of the Spirit are given to both men and women and are to be used for the body of Christ. Restricting women to only teaching women and children deprives the body of Christ of gifts given to mature it.

Of course the Bible must be taken seriously as the word of God so these passages need some explanation. The best explanation I have found regarding 1 Tim 2.12 is that this verse must be understood within the context of the whole book. First Timothy is focused on problems that the church was having with false teachers (e.g., 1 Tim 4:1). Potentially a false teaching had arisen that claimed that Eve was created before Adam. It may well have involved a distortion of the structure of the family. This is opposed in 1 Tim 2:12. One verse alone is insufficient to frame a doctrine. In fact, the teaching of the New Testament must be consistent with the practices of the early church.

There is an example of a woman (Priscilla) teaching a man in Acts 18:26. "He [Apollos] had been instructed in the way of the Lord. And being fervent in spirit, he spoke and taught accurately the things concerning Jesus, though he knew only the baptism of John. He began to speak boldly in the synagogue, but when Priscilla and Aquila heard him, they took him aside and explained to him the way of God more accurately" (Acts 18:25–26). The word "explained" is used of Paul when he explained about the kingdom of God and persuaded people about Jesus (Acts 28:23). It is effectively a synonym for teaching. Those who argue that women can teach men in private and not in public worship are producing a false dichotomy between public and private, as if the way the church worshipped in the New Testament was the same as the present day institutional church. This is not so. The meetings of the early church were in homes. Additionally, it is wrong to make the distinction between teaching one man and teaching many. What would be the cut off number? When two or three are gathered together, Jesus is in the midst (Matt 18:20).

The other issue with the statement in 1 Tim 2:12 is the word translated as "authority" (*authentein*). This word is used only once in the New Testament, making it difficult to know precisely what is meant here. In earlier, non-biblical Greek writings it means someone who does something by his own hand, or the actual or authentic murderer. Paul is most likely not using the word in that way but using it as "autocrat." Jesus told us to exercise authority through service (Matt 20:25–26). But these women were apparently trying to dictate to men, insisting that this was their right since Eve was made first and Adam second. This sounds like a first-century version of radical feminism. If this interpretation is correct, it is not forbidding the exercise of godly authority but instead forbidding the exercise of unbiblical authority in an autocratic fashion.

Some people believe that women should not teach men, and yet they may teach teenagers, who are biblically considered men since they are over the age of thirteen. Others believe that it is acceptable for women to teach men as long as doctrine is not taught. Many have argued that women can teach Sunday school but not adults. Some take no issue with women writing books but object to them speaking those same words in a church service. There is a lot of inconsistent teaching based on this one verse. In my opinion, this verse is not a restriction on women teaching the truth but only a restriction against false teaching and ungodly use of authority.

Jesus taught the people about the kingdom of God. The early church taught about Jesus, his death, and his resurrection. Teaching is very important gift and those who are given it by the Spirit should be encouraged to exercise it regularly in public, in private, in speaking, and in writing. Without good teaching about Jesus, about the kingdom of God, and about Christian living, the church will be ineffective in their witness to Jesus or lead astray by false teaching. Both men and women should be free to exercise this gift in every possible setting, both inside and outside the church.

10

Exhortation/Encouragement

"Having gifts that differ according to the grace given to us,
let us use them . . . *the one who exhorts, in his exhortation*"
(Rom 12:6a, 8a).

MANY SPIRITUAL GIFTS OVERLAP with one another. This is true of prophecy and exhortation/encouragement (encouragement and exhortation are translations of the same Greek word). Prophecy is a gift given for the encouragement of the church (1 Cor 14:3). The use of other gifts should encourage the church as well. Yet exhortation is listed in Rom 12:8 as a distinct gift, different from prophecy.

The word translated "exhortation" can have several different meanings: encouragement, comfort, consolation, appeal, urging, exhortation, and entreaty. Because the word can mean different things, the gift may be exercised in different situations and in different ways, depending on the need. In some settings, the church requires a push to do what is right and in others there is a need for people to be encouraged to continue steadfastly. Sometimes comfort is what is required.

In the Gospels, the word is used several times, but only a couple of instances are connected to the gift. When Jesus was brought to the temple to be dedicated to God as an infant, a man there named Simeon was "waiting for the consolation of Israel" (Luke 2:25). The consolation of Israel was anticipated by the prophecies of Isaiah. He declares, "Comfort, comfort my people, says your God. Speak tenderly to Jerusalem, and cry to her that her warfare is ended, that her iniquity is pardoned, that she has received from the LORD's hand double for all her sins" (Isa 40:1–2). And again in Isa 52:9, "Break forth together into singing, you waste places of Jerusalem, for the LORD has comforted his people; he has redeemed Jerusalem." Simeon recognized that the infant Jesus was the longed-for Messiah, who had come to bring forgiveness of sin and the redemption of Jerusalem (Luke 2:28–32). This firmly places the word in the context of the gospel. In this respect, it is no different from the other gifts, which are all ultimately about the gospel and used to concretely proclaim it. The word is also found in the Sermon on the Mount, in which Jesus tells the people how to live within the kingdom of God. "Blessed are those who mourn, for they shall be *comforted*" (Matt 5:4). Comfort comes to the hurting because the Messiah has come to rule over the kingdom of God.

The Holy Spirit is called the *paraklētos* (John 14:16, 26; 15:26; 16:7), a word connected to the Greek verb "encourage" (*parakaleō*) and noun "encouragement" (*paraklēsis*). This word may be translated in a variety of ways—one who is called on to provide guidance or encouragement, counselor, encourager, helper, intercessor, advocate, one called to speak on behalf of the accused, summoned to one's side, one who helps by consoling or mediating or encouraging, comforter. Jesus is also called the *paraklētos* (1 John 2:1). The source of our encouragement and comfort is always Jesus and the Spirit he has given us in his place. We must not think that our encouragement comes principally from events in life or material goods. They have a purpose, but the real source, the first source, of encouragement is Jesus. The Holy Spirit, then, gives us the encouragement that comes from Jesus since the Spirit's task is to always direct us back to the person of Jesus, what he said, and what he did (John 14:26; 15:26; 16:12–15).

In Acts, the words "encourage" and "encouragement" are used repeatedly. Barnabas had a gift of encouragement. His name was given to him by the apostles and means "son of encouragement" (Acts 4:36). The church experienced the encouragement of the Holy Spirit and grew in number (Acts 9:31). There is no indication as to how the Holy Spirit encouraged the church, but possibly he worked through people who had the gift of encouragement. Barnabas exhorted the church to remain faithful to the Lord (Acts 11:23). Paul and Barnabas together did something similar, reminding the disciples in Lystra, Iconium, and Antioch that they must go through many hardships to enter the kingdom of God (Acts 14:22). Judas and Silas, both prophets, encouraged the Christians in Antioch (Acts 15:32). Paul encouraged the disciples in Ephesus before he left there (Acts 20:1).

Encouragement was also used outside of the church. The sermon at Pentecost includes an exhortation to those outside the church: "Save yourselves from this crooked generation" (Acts 2:40b). In Pisidian Antioch, Barnabas and Saul went to the synagogue and were asked if they had any word of encouragement (Acts 13:14–15). Paul's response to this query was to preach about the history of Israel leading up to the birth of Jesus, who is the anticipated Messiah. He then told them that Jesus came to bring salvation, and went into detail about his death and resurrection. Finally, he exhorted them to believe the message about Jesus lest they become like scoffers who perish (Acts 13:16–41). Paul's encouragement to the Jews was to proclaim the gospel to them and to exhort them to believe. "Beware, therefore, lest what is said in the Prophets should come about: 'Look, you scoffers, be astounded and perish'" (Acts 13:40–41a). These words lead me to conclude that encouragement does not necessarily involve happy words but can include serious exhortation. Another example of encouragement used outside the church is found in Acts 27. Paul was onboard a ship, being taken to Rome, and the ship was being battered by a severe storm. He had received a word from God, through an angel, that they would not perish, because he had to stand trial before Caesar (Acts 27:23–24). Therefore, when the crew had all but given up hope, Paul urged (exhorted) the crew to eat (Acts 27:33–34).

There are many instances in the epistles where "encourage" means "urge" or "appeal." For example, "I appeal to you therefore, brothers, by the mercies of God, to present your bodies as a living sacrifice, holy and acceptable to God, which is your spiritual worship" (Rom 12:1). Paul continually appeals to churches to be obedient to Jesus as a consequence of the gospel (e.g., Rom 15:30; 16:17; 1 Cor 1:10; 2 Cor 2:8). Therefore, at least one aspect of the gift of encouragement is exhorting believers to be obedient to Jesus. An exhortation is not given as a command, but for Paul there was an expectation that those who read his letters would do what he urged them to do. This is because the exhortations were an outworking of the gospel. He urged Christians to act as if they believed the gospel. Acting in accordance with the gospel is a consequence or evidence of faith. Someone with the gift of encouragement may exhort others to do what is godly, holy, and right. This is much more than simply saying "nice" things to encourage someone. In fact, the exhortations can be very serious and even difficult or painful (Heb 12:5–6).

The word can mean "comfort." In many places, the Bible speaks of God comforting his people. "Blessed be the God and Father of our Lord Jesus Christ, the Father of mercies and God of all comfort, who comforts us in all our affliction, so that we may be able to comfort those who are in any affliction, with the comfort with which we ourselves are comforted by God" (2 Cor 1:3–4). Paul was comforted by the comfort God gave through others (2 Cor 7:6–7) and observed God's comfort of others (2 Cor 7:13). Actions done in love provide comfort (Phlm 1:7), although the ultimate source of comfort is the eternal comfort that flows out of God's grace to us in Christ (2 Thess 2:16). So the gift of exhortation/encouragement may involve comforting others when they are experiencing great difficulty, grief, or sorrow. Providing comfort in these situations must include reminding the person of hope found in Christ and the joy that comes from that hope.

Encouragement will likely draw on the Scriptures. Paul reminds us: "For whatever was written in former days was written for our instruction, that through endurance and through the encouragement of the Scriptures we might have hope" (Rom 15:4; see also 1 Thess 4:18). Specifically, encouragement finds its source in Christ (Phil 2:1) and God our Father (2 Thess 2:16). Encouragement must never involve deceit or falsehood (1 Thess 2:3). Love does not lie. Instead, we are encouraged to have hope because of the faithful and truthful character of God (Heb 6:18). Having been encouraged (or comforted) by God, the person is then able to encourage (or comfort) others (2 Cor 1:3–4). The implication here is that the spiritual gift of encouragement will be considerably enhanced by knowledge of the Scriptures, a deep relationship with God, faith in God's faithfulness, and the experience of being encouraged or comforted by God in difficulty. Gifts are not simply given in full measure. Each is grown; choices we make and disciplines we participate in can make a real difference to the effectiveness of the gift. Events in life, which are experienced within the sovereignty of God, are also means of growing our gifts. The gift is given by the Holy Spirit and grows more effective according to the inputs the person receives.

Developing relationships is very important for those who want to exercise a gift of encouragement. On several occasions the Scriptures tell us that people physically went to the churches in order to encourage them (Eph 6:22; Col 4:8; 1 Thess 3:2). Heb 10:24–25 insists that Christians must meet together in order to encourage one another. "And let us consider how to stir up one another to love and good works, not neglecting to meet together, as is the habit of some, but encouraging one another, and all the more as you see the Day drawing near." Exhortation may help two believers to have a better relationship (Phil 4:2). Additionally, those believers who are younger (in years or spiritual maturity) should exhort rather than rebuke older believers (1 Tim 5:1). This keeps respect in the relationship.

And lastly, the purpose of encouragement (or exhortation or comfort) is spelled out in Col 2:1–3. "For I want you to know how great a struggle I have for you and for those at Laodicea and for all who have not seen me face to face, that their hearts may be encouraged, being knit together in love, to reach all the riches of full assurance of understanding and the knowledge of God's mystery, which is Christ, in whom are hidden all the treasures of wisdom and knowledge." God's desire is that we be encouraged in order to know the riches of the mystery, that is, Christ. The gospel is the ultimate content of encouragement (and indeed the basis of every gift). If the encouragement given does not lead to an increased knowledge of Christ or an increased desire to know Christ, then it is not the spiritual gift of encouragement. Encouragement (or exhortation or comfort) is not given to boost self esteem or make people feel good. It has a spiritual purpose and this must be the focus of encouragement. This does not mean that it has to state a generalized gospel message but rather that it must point to the gospel, which is itself deep and wide.

The gift of encouragement has many facets, including encouraging, exhorting, and comforting. The primary comfort or encouragement God offers to his people is his salvation brought about through Jesus. The church is strengthened to be faithful through people with this gift. Encouragement does not have to be "nice" but can be strongly worded. Christians are often exhorted to obedience, and unbelievers are exhorted to repentance. Those who encourage will point the body of Christ to Jesus himself because all that encourages and comforts is found in him and proclaimed in the gospel.

11

Contributing

"Having gifts that differ according to the grace given to us,
let us use them . . . *the one who contributes, in generosity*"
(Rom 12:6a, 8b).

CONTRIBUTING IS A GIFT that seems to be rarely spoken about. Perhaps this gift is not so eagerly sought out because it is not as exciting as the more "supernatural" gifts like healing or miracles. However, the idea of generous giving to others is so countercultural that giving must in fact be a gift of the Spirit. The word itself is not used many times in the New Testament. The concept, however, is a different matter.

John the Baptist used the word "contribute" (found in Rom 12:8) when he explained to the crowds how they could show evidence of repentance for baptism, "Whoever has two tunics is to *share* with him who has none, and whoever has food is to do likewise" (Luke 3:11). Jesus used a synonym when he told the Pharisees to stop obsessing about external things that don't matter and instead "give as alms those things that are within, and behold, everything is clean for you" (Luke 11:41). In the Sermon on the Mount he said, "Give to the one who begs from you, and do not refuse the one who would borrow from you" (Matt 5:42). In fact, giving to those in need is one criterion by which Jesus will judge the nations (Matt 25:35, 42). These passages imply that giving to others is required of all Christians since the Christian life is marked by a Spirit-directed concern for the needs of others.

The gift described in Rom 12:8, then, must go beyond what is expected of all believers. In the current cultural climate of the church, it is not difficult to stand out as a person who gives since the statistics would suggest that Christians are not giving very much by way of money or goods. We seem to have acclimatized ourselves to our greedy and narcissistic culture. However, the gift of contributing generously involves more than simply being obedient to the words of Jesus regarding giving.

It is the nature of God to be outrageously generous. God has no need of anything from creatures but is the source of all for humans. He gives us life, breath, and everything else (Acts 17:25). He gives humans sun, rain, crops, and all the other things we enjoy (Acts 14:17). Everything that is good has its source in him (Jas 1:17). God is far better at giving than the fathers of the world, and even they know how to give to their children (Matt 7:11). But the generosity of God goes well beyond providing us with life and material things. He did not spare his own Son but gave him up for us because he loves us so much. Therefore, he gives believers all things (John 3:16; Rom 8:32). There can be no more generous gift than to give your most beloved Son in order to redeem sinners. Yet God's giving to us extends even further than this. Not only did he give up his only Son for us, he also gives us the gift of his Holy Spirit (Acts 2:38; 8:20; 10:45), as Jesus promised (John 14:16). His love given to believers is shown by making us children of God (1 John 3:1). His other gifts include salvation (Eph 2:8), justification, righteousness (Rom 5:16–17), and grace (Eph 3:7; 4:7).

As we might expect, the gift of contributing generously was exercised in the life of Jesus. There is very little in the Gospels to suggest that Jesus had much by way of money to give to others. He did have a money bag designated for giving to the poor (John 12:6). Being a pious Jew he probably gave to the temple and tithed, although there is no direct evidence of this. However, the gift of contributing in the life of Jesus is broader than giving money. As the Son of God, he was eternally in the presence of the Father and gave up that glory in order to become a human being. Even then, his status was that of the lowest category of humans in the ancient world, a slave (Phil 2:6–7). He was rich and yet he became poor for our sakes, so that we might become rich (2 Cor 8:9). His gave even his own life. "Greater love has no one than this, that someone lay down his life for his friends" (John 15:13). He gave his flesh for the life of the world (John 6:51). But Jesus did not cease to give when his earthly life ended. Ephesians 4:8 tells us, "When he ascended on high he led a host of captives, and he gave gifts to men."

Even from heaven Jesus continues to give generously. This is the kind of outrageously generous giving that the gift of contributing suggests.

It is possible that some churches are generous contributors in a corporate sense. This seems to be the case with the Philippian church and also with the churches in Macedonia. Paul wrote to the Philippians about their generosity:

> I rejoiced in the Lord greatly that now at length you have revived your concern for me. You were indeed concerned for me, but you had no opportunity . . . Yet it was kind of you to share my trouble. And you Philippians yourselves know that in the beginning of the gospel, when I left Macedonia, no church entered into partnership with me in giving and receiving, except you only. Even in Thessalonica you sent me help for my needs once and again. Not that I seek the gift, but I seek the fruit that increases to your credit. I have received full payment, and more. I am well supplied, having received from Epaphroditus the gifts you sent, a fragrant offering, a sacrifice acceptable and pleasing to God (Phil 4:10, 14–18).

The Philippian church was the only church that took care of Paul's needs. As a church they gave several times. It is interesting that a church is given credit for meeting Paul's needs, not an individual with a gift of contributing. Perhaps the church as a whole had a gift of contributing.

The Macedonian churches also gave more than they could reasonably give.

> We want you to know, brothers, about the grace of God that has been given among the churches of Macedonia, for in a severe test of affliction, their abundance of joy and their extreme poverty have overflowed in a wealth of generosity on their part. For they gave according to their means, as I can testify, and beyond their means, of their own accord, begging us earnestly for the favor of taking part in the relief of the saints—and this, not as we expected, but they gave themselves first to the Lord and then by the will of God to us (2 Cor 8:1–5).

Again it seems that the church as a whole was extraordinarily generous. They were commended because they gave out of their extreme poverty. Their actions were quite contrary to logic. If you already have too little to meet your own needs, then why would you give that away in order to meet someone else's needs? This generosity must surely be an outworking of the gospel and the empowering of the Holy Spirit. But the point here is that it seems that the church, not just individuals, had this gift.

How does the gift operate? Those who have been stealing are exhorted to do something useful so as to have something to *share* with others in need (Eph 4:28). "Share" is the same word as the gift of "contributing." This suggests that the gift operates through the natural means of working, earning, and giving. Paul explained that he worked hard to supply his own needs and the needs of others (Acts 20:34). Possibly those people who are inclined to self-employment may be more likely to have the gift since they have more flexible means of gaining income than employees. However, it may not be so. Anyone can give generously from the income he or she has, even if that income does not grow. But perhaps the desire to give generously will also be accompanied by creativity to produce more income in order to share. I am reminded of a story my father-in-law once told me. A particular man was told by the Spirit to purchase a lottery ticket. The ticket cost $1. Each week, for months and months, the man won various amounts of money in the lottery, and gave away all the money to missions, only keeping $1 to buy another ticket. When one week he did not win any money, he stopped buying lottery tickets. This is certainly a creative way of acquiring money to give to others.

But contributing is not confined to money. Jesus gave of himself, and others in the Bible are said to do the same. "So, being affectionately desirous of you, we were ready to *share* with you not only the gospel of God but also our own selves, because you had become very dear to us" (1 Thess 2:8). So it is not just money that is given but also lives and the gospel. Paul commends the Galatians for being so generous that they would have torn out their own eyes and given them to him if that were possible (Gal 4:15).

According to Rom 12:8, those who have the gift of contributing must give generously. The word translated here as "generous" can mean "simplicity of heart" or "integrity." Another way of putting this is to give with unmixed motivation. It is possible to give money with all kinds of motivations. If a person gives in public view of others, the motivation may well be personal glory. Giving can oil the wheels of commerce or it can be used to bribe others. Giving may be done in order to seem pious before God. In the "love chapter," 1 Cor 13, Paul reminds people that giving must be motivated solely by love. "If I give away all I have, and if I deliver up my body to be burned, but have not love, I gain nothing" (1 Cor 13:3). So the injunction of Rom 12:8 to give generously is put there as a caution against giving with a motivation other than love.

Because of this danger, it is best to avoid giving too publicly. Some gifts are out in the open and can easily be seen by others. The gift of generous contributing may not be open to scrutiny at all. Jesus told us, "Thus, when you give to the needy, sound no trumpet before you, as the hypocrites do in the synagogues and in the streets, that they may be praised by others. Truly, I say to you, they have received their reward. But when you give to the needy, do not let your left hand know what your right hand is doing, so that your giving may be in secret. And your Father who sees in secret will reward you" (Matt 6:2–4). Therefore, contributing may need to be done discretely and even secretly. This is clearly not always the case since we know about the churches that gave generously (see above). But it is not something to announce loudly in church.

Matthew 6:2–4 also suggests that there is a counterfeit gift contributing, just as there are other counterfeit gifts (prophecy, teaching, miracles etc.). The counterfeit looks like the opposite of the true because it announces itself in order to look spiritual, while in fact being deceitful. A couple of biblical examples can make this clear. When Jesus was anointed at Bethany with expensive perfume (John 12:1–8), Judas spoke up. "Why was this ointment not sold for three hundred denarii and given to the poor?" (v. 5). On the surface this looks like someone who wanted to give generously to the poor. But the truth was otherwise. "He said this, not because he cared about the poor, but because he was a thief, and having charge of the moneybag he used to help himself to what was put into it" (v. 6). In Acts 5:1–11, there is another example of counterfeit giving. Since many in the Jerusalem church had been selling their property and giving this to the apostles to distribute to the needy, Ananias and Sapphira thought that they could look good by saying that they had done the same. But they lied, and died as a result.

Matthew 6:2–4 states that generous giving will be rewarded. Some people preach that if you give, then you will gain financially, that giving is the path to becoming rich. However, this is not the biblical picture. It may be that God gives more money to those who give generously in order that they can give more generously. Instead of increase in money, the Bible promises an increase in righteousness and thanksgiving to God (2 Cor 9:10–11).

In regard to the question of whether this gift is to be used inside or outside the church, I think that there is definitely potential to use it outside the church, but I cannot find examples of this in the Bible. Jesus gave his own life when there was no church, so the gift of contributing does not require a church in order to be used. But the other examples in the New Testament seem to be internal, not external. Historically the church has given generously to the poor and the weak outside the church, in founding hospitals, orphanages, and schools etc. This strongly suggests that contributing may be used to demonstrate to the lost world the generosity of God in the gospel.

The God and Father of our Lord Jesus Christ is a generous God. This generosity is evident in the self-giving love of Jesus. The gift of contributing generously may not be popularly sought after, but it is a significant gift. Generous giving is the means by which God meets the needs of his people. It is also the means by which kingdom work is financed. All this may be invisible to others, but giving generously is never invisible to God. People with this gift can be assured that their contributing will give glory to God.

12

Leading

"Having gifts that differ according to the grace given to us, let us use them . . . *the one who leads, with zeal*" (Rom 12:6a, 8c).

THE BIBLICAL GIFT OF leading should not be confused with the leadership model presented by culture. Although the church in Australia (and elsewhere) seems more and more to be adopting a leadership model similar to the culture, this is the wrong pattern to be following. The cultural model is centered on business and administration, but biblical leadership is centered on the family pattern or the pattern of shepherd and sheep. Let us begin with the life of Jesus and his work as the good shepherd of the sheep.

Jesus' life is the pattern for the Christian life, so we can understand the gift of shepherding or leading by first looking at what Jesus did. Jesus is the shepherd of Israel, the one about whom Micah prophesied. "And you, O Bethlehem, in the land of Judah, are by no means least among the rulers of Judah; for from you will come a ruler who will shepherd my people Israel" (Matt 2:6, quoting Mic 5:2–4). In his days on earth, Jesus acted like a shepherd and the people of Israel were his sheep. Jesus taught the crowds about the kingdom of God and healed the sick (Matt 9:35; Mark 6:34) "because they were harassed and helpless, like sheep without a shepherd" (Matt 9:36). Teaching people and meeting their needs is a significant part of biblical shepherding.

Jesus said,

> I am the good shepherd. The good shepherd lays down his life for the sheep. He who is a hired hand and not a shepherd, who does not own the sheep, sees the wolf coming and leaves the sheep and flees, and the wolf snatches them and scatters them. He flees because he is a hired hand and cares nothing for the sheep. I am the good shepherd. I know my own and my own know me, just as the Father knows me and I know the Father; and I lay down my life for the sheep. And I have other sheep that are not of this fold. I must bring them also, and they will listen to my voice. So there will be one flock, one shepherd (John 10:11–16).

Shepherding is first of all self-sacrificing. Jesus, the good shepherd, gave his own life for the sake of the flock. This is contrary to the idea that leadership gains glory for the leader. Second, without leaders the flock is very vulnerable to wolves. A great many negative influences, spiritual forces, and antagonistic people are against the church. If there are no shepherds to keep the flock safe, then the church will be hurt, scattered, and ineffective in the world. Third, there is one flock and one shepherd, not multiple flocks. The church is pastored in many different locations, but we are all one flock.

Although the flock of God is first of all shepherded by Jesus, who is "the great shepherd of the sheep" (Heb 13:20) and "the Shepherd and Overseer" of our souls (1 Pet 2:25), the leaders of the church are under-shepherds of the flock. After his resurrection, Jesus gave Peter the instruction, "Tend my sheep" (John 21:16). Paul exhorted the Ephesian elders to "Pay careful attention to yourselves and to all the flock, in which the Holy Spirit has made you overseers, to care for the church of God, which he obtained with his own blood" (Acts 20:28). The sheep belong to Jesus, but he does not merely shepherd them from heaven. Jesus appoints people to shepherd his flock. As with the other things Jesus is doing in the world, he is taking care of his church through people.

Leadership in the church has leadership in the family as its model. Anyone who would be an overseer "must *manage* his own household well, with all dignity keeping his children submissive, for if someone does not know how to *manage* his own household, how will he care for God's church?" (1 Tim 3:4–5). A very similar instruction is given in 1 Tim 3:12. "Let deacons each be the husband of one wife, *managing* their children and their own households well." Leading is used in 3:4–5 as a synonym for caring. In other words, Christian leadership is caring for the church. It is not about lording it over others or having power over one another. In fact, Jesus himself made this point when he told the disciples who wanted to hold positions of power in the kingdom of God, "You know that the rulers of the Gentiles lord it over them, and their great ones exercise authority over them. It shall not be so among you. But whoever would be great among you must be your servant, and whoever would be first among you must be your slave" (Matt 20:25–27).

Leadership as caring for the church fits well with the idea of shepherding discussed above. The shepherd makes sure that the sheep are well fed, watered, and kept safe from harm. The shepherd leads the sheep and the sheep follow the shepherd. There is no need for coercion because the sheep learn to trust the shepherd. The good shepherd does not harm the sheep or neglect the sheep due to laziness or cowardice. Church leaders are not people in positions of power over others, but servants who give of themselves for the sake of seeing the church mature and become Christ-like. Caring is an other-centered activity. Just as Jesus gave his life for his flock, so too those who would lead the church need to have their focus on caring for the flock at the expense of their own interests.

Let's further consider the family model in order to understand how the gift of leading works in the church. There are several "household codes" in the New Testament. The New Testament household would have included husband, wife, children, and possibly slaves. Ephesians 5:21–6:9 describes three kinds of leadership: husbands leading wives, parents leading children, and masters leading slaves. Husbands are to loves their wives by following the example of Christ who gave himself for his bride, the church (Eph 5:25). This works out in marriage in the instruction, "In the same way husbands should love their wives as their own bodies" (Eph 5:28). This kind of leadership is both sacrificial and values the other person as much as oneself.

In the case of parents leading children, the parent has real authority over the child, but this is to be used lovingly and carefully. "Fathers, do not provoke your children to anger, but bring them up in the discipline and instruction of the Lord" (Eph 6:4). In theory, the father in the household could merely command the children to obey him and expect that this would occur. Yet he is instructed to make sure that the commands he gives are not arbitrary and inconsiderate. The goal of parenting is not control over children but training and instruction in order that the child become godly. The goal of leadership is to gently train people for godliness.

The third relationship is that of masters and slaves. The master had every "right" to control the slave. But instead, masters are told to "do the same to them, and stop your threatening, knowing that he who is both their

Master and yours is in heaven, and that there is no partiality with him" (Eph 6:9). Masters must remember that they also have a master to whom they are accountable. Leaders, then, need also to remember to whom they must give an account of their leadership.

Another very significant passage to do with leading is 1 Thess 5:12. "We ask you, brothers, to respect those who labor among you and are over you [lead you] in the Lord and admonish you." The three activities mentioned in this verse are quite likely connected together. Church leaders are the ones who labor among believers, who are over them, and who admonish. If we accept that leading involves these things, then some very interesting conclusions follow. The first of which is the somewhat surprising conclusion that the New Testament mentions several women in leadership positions in the early church. Several women are explicitly mentioned as those who labor in the Lord. Romans 16 mentions four women in this category: Mary (v. 6), Tryphena, Tryphosa, and Persis (v. 12). First Corinthians 16 also mentions women in leadership, but less explicitly. "Now I urge you, brothers—you know that the household of Stephanas were the first converts in Achaia, and that they have devoted themselves to the service of the saints—be subject to such as these, and to every fellow worker and laborer" (1 Cor 16:15–16). The household of Stephanas would no doubt have included his wife and possibly children and slaves. These people are commended as those who served the saints. Indeed, the Corinthians were instructed to submit to them and anyone else who is involved in this labor. It is clear that this instruction tells the church to submit to the leadership of at least one woman. The word "submit" is the same word used of "wives, submit to your own husbands, as to the Lord" (Eph 5:22).

Several passages explain what laboring involves. It involves working hard for the weak (Acts 20:35), preaching the gospel (1 Cor 15:9–11), serving the saints (1 Cor 16:15–16), working to disciple the church (Gal 4:11; Phil 2:16), self-sacrifice (Phil 2:17), teaching and admonishing the church so that each person would become mature in Christ (Col 1:28–29), and often preaching and teaching (1 Tim 5:17). Admonishing has a similar goal to laboring (Col 1:28). The aim is to see the church mature and become obedient to the gospel. Based on my earlier conclusion about women in leadership, I believe that these activities were also conducted by women in the early church.

Leadership requires character qualities in order to be effective. Those who lead must "be above reproach, the husband of one wife, sober-minded, self-controlled, respectable, hospitable, able to teach" (1 Tim 3:2), "not be arrogant or quick-tempered or a drunkard or violent or greedy for gain" (Titus 1:7). Without appropriate character qualities, the leader may well be swayed by being in a position of authority. For this reason a leader must not be a new convert (1 Tim 3:6). This suggests that the gift of leadership needs to be used in ever increasing increments. This way the person can have opportunity to grow in the gift, while at the same time developing the character qualities needed to accompany the exercise of it. Gifts must be exercised in love. Leading comes with its own unique temptations, so in order to use the gift in love the person must learn how to use the gift carefully.

Although we might naturally think of leadership as coming with privilege, the Christian leader is likely to experience suffering and be required to give all of himself or herself to others through service. This might put people off exercising the gift. Therefore, those who lead are instructed to do so zealously (Rom 12:8), diligently, and enthusiastically, making every effort to do it well. The apostle Peter reminds those who shepherd the flock of God that they should do so willingly, not because they must. The motivation that he gives for this task is the glory that will be revealed when Jesus returns (1 Pet 5:1–3). "And when the Chief Shepherd appears, you will receive the unfading crown of glory" (1 Pet 5:4). So it is not the fading glory of being in the spotlight or the privilege of being important that should motivate Christian leaders, but a perspective on eternity.

As with several other gifts, there is a false version of the gift. There is no doubt that many people who do not know Jesus have real charisma and people follow them. Quite often such people can take control of churches. Jude mentions this kind of leader in his letter. "These are hidden reefs at your love feasts, as they feast with you without fear, shepherds feeding themselves; waterless clouds, swept along by winds; fruitless trees in late autumn, twice dead, uprooted" (Jude 1:12). The flock of God can be led astray into doing what is wrong by people with this false (that is, not from the Holy Spirit) gift of leadership. Those exercising the false gift often start cults and have faithful followers, who are deluded into thinking that they are serving God. This makes the false gift of leading very dangerous to the church. We should watch out for it. The way to tell the difference is to know what the real thing looks like. The false will focus on the person who leads. The true leader will bring the focus of the church onto Jesus and away from the person who leads.

There are few examples in the New Testament of this gift being exercised outside of the church. In the ministry of Jesus there was as yet no church, so when Jesus led the people, he led those who were outside the church in order that they would become his church. His death was the ultimate act of sacrificial leadership and made the church possible. The work of Christian leaders spreading the gospel in order to get people into the church is an example of leadership outside the church. Although this overlaps with the gift of evangelism, there is a difference between evangelism by individuals without leadership gifts and evangelism by those with leadership gifts. Leaders do not simply evangelize and pass the convert over to another. Leaders make sure that the new convert is securely anchored in the faith and cared for.

On the other hand, Jesus is ruler or shepherd to both those inside the church and those outside. He is a positive ruler or caring shepherd to those who follow him and worship him. "For the Lamb in the midst of the throne will be their shepherd, and he will guide them to springs of living water, and God will wipe away every tear from their eyes" (Rev 7:17). Here the shepherding (or ruling) of Jesus is benevolent towards his people. But the same verb is used to describe Jesus with respect to those who refuse his lordship. "She [Israel] gave birth to a male child, one who is to *rule* all the nations with a rod of iron, but her child was caught up to God and to his throne" (Rev 12:5). And elsewhere we are told, "From his [Jesus'] mouth comes a sharp sword with which to strike down the nations, and he will *rule* them with a rod of iron. He will tread the winepress of the fury of the wrath of God the Almighty" (Rev 19:15). The words "shepherd" and "rule" used in these verses are translations of the same Greek word. In the latter two verses, Jesus is not benevolent towards those who will not obey him. His leadership over them will strike fear into his enemies.

Although leadership should never be anything like that exercised by the secular culture, within the sphere of those who are outside the church it can and must be forceful. I use forceful here, not in the sense of violent, but in the sense of exercising clear authority. The authority of the gospel gives the disciples of Jesus the mandate to make clear the consequences of refusing the gentle shepherding of Jesus. Jesus will rule the individual one way or the other. He is lord. The task of Christian leaders towards the nonbelieving world is to help people to see that there is a real consequence to rejecting the benevolent leading of Jesus. The consequence is that Jesus will "rule with a rod of iron" over those who refuse him.

In the church leading is shepherding, caring for the sheep. The sheep belong to Jesus, the Great Shepherd, so leaders must act like people who will give an account of their actions. The church is like a family. The goal of leading is not fame or power but nurturing, guiding, training, and keeping the church safe. It involves costly self-sacrifice, but the reward is glory at the return of Jesus. The church truly needs leaders who are willing to provide Christ-like leadership. Without godly leadership, the people of God will fall prey to wolves.

13

Acts of Mercy

"Having gifts that differ according to the grace given to us, let us use them . . . the one who does acts of mercy, with cheerfulness" (Rom 12:6a, 8d).

MERCY IS A CHARACTER quality, but it is also listed as a gift of the Spirit. Before I began this study, I thought that acts of mercy were feeding the hungry and clothing the naked. Although I still believe that these are acts of mercy, I have found something far deeper in working through the biblical material on mercy.

Mercy begins with God and specifically with his faithfulness to his covenant with Israel. In the first chapter of Luke there are two important prophetic "songs": the Song of Mary (*Magnificat*) and the Song of Zechariah (*Benedictus*). Both mention the mercy of God towards his people. "And Mary said, 'My soul magnifies the Lord, and my spirit rejoices in God my Savior . . . And his *mercy* is for those who fear him from generation to generation . . . He has helped his servant Israel, in remembrance of his *mercy*, as he spoke to our fathers, to Abraham and to his offspring forever'" (Luke 1:46–47, 50, 54–55). God's mercy is mentioned twice in this song and explored in its content. God has performed mighty deeds, opposed the proud, brought rulers to nothing, lifted up the humble, filled the hungry, but made the rich empty. God's mercy is shown to his people in accordance with his promises.

Zechariah also speaks of God's mercy. "'Blessed be the Lord God of Israel, for he has visited and redeemed his people . . . to show the *mercy* promised to our fathers and to remember his holy covenant . . . because of the tender *mercy* of our God, whereby the sunrise shall visit us from on high to give light to those who sit in darkness and in the shadow of death, to guide our feet into the way of peace'" (Luke 1:68, 72, 78–79). In Zechariah's Song, mercy is clearly connected with God's covenant with Israel. When God shows mercy to his people he is remembering his covenant and offering forgiveness of sins and salvation.

Therefore, mercy begins with God, particularly with his most significant act of redemption, sending his Son into the world to save sinners. Understanding the gift of mercy, then, does not begin with human acts of kindness but with God. We cannot show the mercy of God without having experienced the mercy of God through Christ. The mercy of Jesus flows through his people to others.

Mercy is a quality of great importance to the Christian life. Jesus said in the Sermon on the Mount, "Blessed are the merciful, for they shall receive mercy" (Matt 5:7). We must be people who are merciful because mercy is characteristic of the way God treats his people. He has been merciful to us and we must be merciful to others. This idea is found in the New Testament, and echoes the preaching of the Old Testament prophets. On two separate occasions in Matthew's Gospel Jesus alludes to Hos 6:6—"I desire mercy, and not sacrifice" (Matt 9:13; 12:7). Mercy is one of the weightier matters of the law, along with justice and faithfulness (Matt 23:23). This brings to mind Mic 6:8—"He has told you, O man, what is good; and what does the LORD require of you but to do justice, and to love kindness, and to walk humbly with your God?"

In both Hos 6:6 and Mic 6:8, the word mercy is a translation of the Hebrew word *hesed* (see also Ps 5:7; 143:12). *Hesed* describes the mutual obligation of covenant relationship. So God treats his people with mercy or kindness because of his covenant with them. Humans are to treat one another with mercy or kindness because they are in relationship with others. This obligation is illustrated in the parable of the Good Samaritan. One day an expert in the law came to Jesus and asked him, "Teacher, what shall I do to inherit eternal life?" (Luke 10:25). Jesus turned the question around and asked him what he thought. The man responded that we must love God and love our neighbor. The story of the Good Samaritan explains who our neighbor is. In the parable, there is only one person who actually acts like a neighbor to the man who was robbed and beaten—the Samaritan. He expressed his obligation to his neighbor by helping him and caring for his needs (Luke 10:25–37). He is "the one who showed him mercy" (Luke 10:37).

During his ministry, many people called out to Jesus for mercy. Two blind men asked for mercy and received their sight (Matt 9:27–30). A Canaanite woman asked Jesus for mercy on her demon-possessed daughter and she was healed (Matt 15:22–28). A man asked Jesus to have mercy on his epileptic son and Jesus cast the demon out (Matt 17:14–18). Another two blind men asked Jesus for mercy and he gave them their sight (Matt 20:30–34). After Jesus healed the demoniac who was inhabited by a legion of demons, he told the man to tell his family and friends about the mercy of God towards him (Mark 5:19). Ten lepers came to Jesus and asked him for mercy and were cleansed of their leprosy (Luke 17:13–14). In two of these stories, it is written that Jesus had compassion on the people. His compassion and his mercy are linked. He healed the sick because of his compassion (Matt 14:14). He fed the hungry because of his compassion towards them (Matt 15:32). He touched and healed a leper because of his compassion (Mark 1:40–41). He taught the crowds because of his compassion towards those who were like sheep without a shepherd (Mark 6:34). He raised the only son of a widow from the dead because he had compassion on her (Luke 7:12–14).

When Jesus had mercy and compassion on people, he healed the sick, fed the hungry, cast out demons, cleansed the lepers, gave sight to the blind, taught the people who were lost, and restored a dead son to his widowed mother. Jesus did not leave people in their sorrow or with their needs unmet. He showed the mercy of God to people by acting to meet human need in whatever form that arose. Acts of mercy, then, are diverse. Mercy meets human needs. In these passages, mercy seems to overlap with healing, miracles, teaching, and exorcism. This does not mean that the gift of mercy necessarily involves those other gifts. Jesus exercised more than one gift at a time. But fundamentally, mercy meets the needs of the hurting.

One fruit of the mercy that finds its ground in God is forgiveness of sin. Jesus told a story about incredible forgiveness in Matt 18:21–35. A man owed an outrageous amount of money to a king. The debt was so great that no one could repay it in many lifetimes. But "out of *pity* for him, the master of that servant released him and forgave him the debt" (v. 27). When the man found a fellow servant who owed him a trivial amount he demanded immediate payment. This resulted in the forgiven servant losing his forgiveness. The explanation: "And should not you have had *mercy* on your fellow servant, as I had *mercy* on you?" (v. 33). In Luke, Jesus tells another story of incredible forgiveness, generally known as the story of the prodigal son. The son returned home and "while he was still a long way off, his father saw him and felt *compassion*, and ran and embraced him and kissed him" (Luke 15:20). In both stories, God is portrayed as being very forgiving. He has mercy and compassion on sinful people as long as they return to him and seek his forgiveness.

Mercy is the counterweight to justice. God requires that his people act justly because he is righteous. But his mercy always balances out his justice. The story of the woman caught in adultery (John 8:2–11) illustrates this. According to the law the woman should have been put to death (Lev 20:10). But the mercy Jesus showed to this woman included setting her free from the just penalty of law and then setting her free from sin. "Neither do I condemn you," Jesus declared, "go, and from now on sin no more" (John 8:11). If Christians are to show the mercy of God to others, then the penalty of law need not always be applied. Mercy can be and must be shown to sinners since as sinners we have had mercy shown to us.

This leads me to suggest that the gift of mercy may involve showing the mercy of God by forgiving the sins of others. Since every Christian is expected to forgive others (Col 3:13), this forgiveness must go beyond the ordinary to be called the gift of mercy. There are examples of Christians who have been able to forgive huge sins against them. One such is in a story told by Miroslav Volf. When he was a child, his younger brother died as a result of the negligence of his nanny (among others). The parents forgave the nanny and continued to employ her. So incredible was this act of forgiveness that Volf had no idea that the nanny was at fault until he was forty-two years old.[1] These kinds of extreme acts of forgiveness are acts of mercy towards sinners and demonstrate the mercy of God.

Mercy may involve simply being with people, befriending people who are not very pleasant, or being present with the lonely. God's mercy extends to his enemies. "For he makes his sun rise on the evil and on the good, and sends rain on the just and on the unjust" (Matt 5:45). Although every Christian is called to show mercy to the unlovable, those whose gift is showing mercy will do this as a matter of course. They will be found making friends with difficult people, even seeking them out.

1. "Exclusion and Embrace." http://www.abc.net.au/radionational/programs/bigideas/exclusion-and-embrace/5331960

Does the gift of mercy operate inside or outside the church? The answer is both. In Mark's Gospel, there are two stories about Jesus feeding multitudes. The first feeding takes place within Jewish territory. The second is outside of Israel. There are differences in the stories because of their different contexts, but they have some things in common. One of these is that Jesus had compassion on the people. "When he went ashore he saw a great crowd, and *he had compassion on them*, because they were like sheep without a shepherd. And he began to teach them many things" (Mark 6:34). "*I have compassion on the crowd*, because they have been with me now three days and have nothing to eat" (Mark 8:2). Jesus had compassion on people inside and outside of Israel. They both needed that compassion. Human needs are present inside and outside the church and these must be met. Mercy towards those who have sinned grievously also applies both inside and outside the church.

God has shown mercy to both the Jew and the Gentile, including both within his plan of salvation (Rom 11:31). The way in which God expressed his immense mercy towards us, because he loved us, was by making alive those who were dead in sin and saving us by grace (Eph 2:4–5). "He saved us, not because of works done by us in righteousness, but according to his own mercy" (Titus 3:5a). Mercy is intrinsically connected with grace and peace (1 Tim 1:2; 2 Tim 1:2; 2 John 1:3). Jesus is a merciful and faithful high priest, who has made propitiation for the sins of the people (Heb 2:7). When we come to God's throne of grace, on the basis of the shed blood of Christ, we can receive mercy and grace from God (Heb 4:14–16). By God's mercy those who believe in Jesus have been born into a living hope (1 Pet 1:3). The mercy of Jesus leads to eternal life (Jude 1:21). Therefore, we are to glorify God for his mercy (Rom 15:8–9).

The way God acts towards sinners and his redeemed people is an indication of what the gift of mercy looks like. Because of his mercy, God has granted believers a ministry that brings righteousness, a ministry of the Spirit (2 Cor 3:7–9; 4:1). He has included us in the wonderful work he is doing for humanity. Paul understood this mercy because he was saved out of a life of persecuting the church and allowed the privilege of being appointed to the service of God (1 Tim 1:12–13). Gentiles must also understand this mercy since they were once not a people but have now become part of God's people through his mercy (1 Pet 2:10).

If the mercy of God enfolds sinners into his family and appoints them to do the work of God, then surely the gift of mercy must find a parallel to this. When people are lost and outside God's purposes, they do not know the glory of having a life of purpose. Mercy includes people within family, within community, within a place of love. Mercy helps people to do something with a purpose, to have meaningful things to do with their lives. Mercy is patient with those who do not understand God's salvation. Practically this involves helping people outside the church, those who are without human connection, without employment, and without a significant grasp of how to do something which matters, to have help to connect, to be employed, and to live a life of significance. This is how mercy may operate outside the church. The mercy of God overflows to sinners, even outside the sphere of salvation.

Finally, those who show mercy must do it cheerfully (Rom 12:8). Why this particular instruction? Acts of mercy may involve being with people at their lowest point. It would be possible to act mercifully and to do so with bitterness or grumpiness. But the instruction is to show mercy with cheerfulness. If mercy is given while being resentful, the action is contradicted by the attitude. Human dignity cannot be upheld by people who resent the actions intended to lift people up. But when acts of mercy are done with cheerfulness, this reinforces the idea that the people who are being helped are actually worth the effort. The value of the person is maintained by the cheerful attitude. It is a good thing, a happy thing, to help those who are vulnerable and weak. Even in the case of forgiving heinous sins, there can supernaturally be cheerfulness, since the attitude of God towards those he forgives in his mercy is a positive one.

The gift of mercy is an overflow of the mercy of God expressed in his covenant with his people. God is merciful to humanity, and believers with the gift of mercy show that mercy to others in concrete ways. Mercy involves meeting human needs in diverse ways. Whenever a person is in a desperate situation, the gift of mercy can be helpful. Mercy can lift people up through showing God's forgiveness in situations of extreme offence. However mercy is expressed, it will declare the gospel in ways that meet the needs of hurting people.

14

Utterance of Wisdom

"For to one is given through the Spirit the utterance of wisdom" (1 Cor 12:8a).

SINCE THE EXPRESSION "UTTERANCE of wisdom" is found only in 1 Cor 12:8, it is necessary to look more widely in the New Testament to understand what this gift entails. I will begin with Jesus, who is himself wisdom.

One of the traditions the Gospels draw on in their portrayal of Jesus is the wisdom tradition. The book of Proverbs speaks of wisdom, who calls out to all humanity to heed her words so that people may gain understanding and knowledge (Prov 8). The New Testament implies that Jesus is personified wisdom. Matthew records Jesus saying, "For John came neither eating nor drinking, and they say, 'He has a demon.' The Son of Man came eating and drinking, and they say, 'Look at him! A glutton and a drunkard, a friend of tax collectors and sinners!' Yet wisdom is justified by her deeds" (Matt 11:18–19). Jesus is the one who does wisdom's deeds. In Matt 11:25–27, Jesus tells us that "these things" are hidden from the wise and learned but revealed through himself, since he alone knows the Father and the Father knows him. In some ways, this is like a description of lady wisdom. Wisdom can only be known by God. Jesus, too, is only known by God the Father and by those who have him revealed to them.

In Matt 11:28–30, Jesus called out, "Come to me, all who labor and are heavy laden, and I will give you rest. Take my yoke upon you, and learn from me, for I am gentle and lowly in heart, and you will find rest for your souls. For my yoke is easy, and my burden is light." This saying is similar to one written about wisdom in Sirach (a book written between the Old Testament and the New)—"Draw near to me, you who are uneducated, and lodge in the house of instruction. Why do you say you are lacking in these things, and why do you endure such great thirst? I opened my mouth and said, Acquire wisdom for yourselves without money. Put your neck under her yoke, and let your souls receive instruction; it is to be found close by. See with your own eyes that I have labored but little and found for myself much serenity" (Sir 51:23–27). In the Sirach passage, wisdom invites people to put their necks under her yoke. In Matthew, it is Jesus who invites people to put on his yoke. The parallel shows that Jesus is wisdom personified.

Another indication that Jesus is wisdom personified is found by comparing Matthew and Luke. In Matt 23:34, Jesus said, "Therefore I send you prophets and wise men and scribes, some of whom you will kill and crucify." In Luke 11:49 there is a similar saying but with a difference: "Therefore also the Wisdom of God said, 'I will send them prophets and apostles, some of whom they will kill and persecute.'" The comparison of the two passages suggests that Jesus is himself the wisdom of God.

It was evident to those who heard and saw him that Jesus had great wisdom (Matt 12:42; 13:54), which he received from the Holy Spirit. Even as a child, Jesus grew and was filled with wisdom (Luke 2:40) because he is the one on whom the Spirit of wisdom and understanding rests (Isa 11:2). Jesus gives his wisdom to those who follow him. When his followers are persecuted, they will witness to Jesus, but have no need to worry about what to say when brought before civil authorities (Luke 21:12–14). "For I will give you a mouth and wisdom, which none of your adversaries will be able to withstand or contradict" (Luke 21:15). This wisdom will be given by the Holy Spirit (Matt 10:20; Mark 13:11). Its purpose is the proclamation of the gospel.

Paul also sees Jesus as wisdom, in marked contrast to the wisdom of the world. "For Jews demand signs and Greeks seek wisdom, but we preach Christ crucified, a stumbling block to Jews and folly to Gentiles, but to those who are called, both Jews and Greeks, *Christ the power of God and the wisdom of God*" (1 Cor 1:22–24). What the world considers wisdom is quite useless when it comes to knowing God. In contrast, the wisdom of God seems utterly foolish to the world. The wisdom of God is shown in the cross, something that makes little sense in terms of worldly wisdom. Jesus is himself the wisdom of God. "And because of him you are in Christ Jesus, *who became to us wisdom from God*, righteousness and sanctification and redemption" (1 Cor 1:30).

The wisdom of this age and the wisdom of God are again contrasted a couple of verses later. "Yet among the mature we do impart wisdom, although it is not a wisdom of this age or of the rulers of this age, who are doomed to pass away. But we impart a secret and hidden wisdom of God, which God decreed before the ages for our glory. None of the rulers of this age understood this, for if they had, they would not have crucified the Lord of glory . . . these things God has revealed to us through the Spirit. For the Spirit searches everything, even the depths of God" (1 Cor 2:6–8, 10). The wisdom of God can only be understood by the mature, those who perceive it in the cross of Jesus. It is a wisdom hidden from the world, those without the Holy Spirit. Only the Spirit knows the depths of God and imparts wisdom to the people of God.

Consequently, the utterance of wisdom must point the church towards Jesus, who is the wisdom of God, and to the cross, where the wisdom of God is displayed. This gift cannot be merely a rehashing of the kind of wisdom that might be found in worldly-wise people. Instead, the Holy Spirit provides wisdom about how to apply the cross to the problem at hand. What this wisdom looks like will in fact often seem strange. "For the foolishness of God is wiser than men, and the weakness of God is stronger than men . . . God chose what is foolish in the world to shame the wise; God chose what is weak in the world to shame the strong" (1 Cor 1:25, 27). Where we might expect power to overcome some problem, God uses the weakness and foolishness of the cross. This, then, is what we should expect as an utterance of wisdom.

Because wisdom is found in the cross, it is not surprising that wisdom is connected to grace and forgiveness. "In [Christ] we have redemption through his blood, the forgiveness of our trespasses, according to the riches of his grace, which he lavished upon us, in all wisdom and insight" (Eph 1:7–8). Offering grace and forgiveness to those who wronged us may seem foolish, but in fact it is what God has done in his wisdom. Wisdom is also connected with the knowledge of God. Paul prayed "that the God of our Lord Jesus Christ, the Father of glory, may give you the Spirit of wisdom and of revelation in the knowledge of him" (Eph 1:17; see also Col 1:9). Those who do not acknowledge God or give thanks to him become fools who think they are wise, and consequently worship idols (Rom 1:21–23). The church is the vessel through which God makes known his wisdom to the rulers and authorities in heavenly places. This is possible because the unsearchable riches of Christ have been made known to the church (Eph 3:8–10). An utterance of wisdom will in some way make known the manifold riches of Christ since in Christ "are hidden all the treasures of wisdom and knowledge" (Col 2:3).

Acts gives us some examples of people who had wisdom from the Holy Spirit. When there was a dispute over food distribution in the early church, it was necessary to appoint some people who were full of the Spirit and wisdom to deal with the situation (Acts 6:1–3). One of these men, Stephen, used his Spirit-given wisdom in other situations. He preached the word, did miracles, and came into conflict with The Synagogue of the Freedmen, who "rose up and disputed with Stephen. But they could not withstand the wisdom and the Spirit with which he was speaking" (Acts 6:9c–10). In the first instance, wisdom was used in an administrative capacity. But in the second, wisdom was something spoken. Spoken wisdom is likely to correspond to what Paul is speaking about in 1 Cor 12:8, where he mentions an utterance of wisdom.

Here are some potential examples of the use of the gift. Paul apparently exercised wisdom when writing his epistles. "And count the patience of our Lord as salvation, just as our beloved brother Paul also wrote to you according to the wisdom given him" (2 Pet 3:15–16). Wisdom is also necessary in interpreting the Scriptures. "This calls for wisdom: let the one who has understanding calculate the number of the beast, for it is the number of a man, and his number is 666" (Rev 13:18). "This calls for a mind with wisdom: the seven heads are seven mountains on which the woman is seated" (Rev 17:9). Paul tells the Corinthians not to go to law courts over disputes between believers. They are to judge within the church. He asks, "I say this to your shame. Can it be that there is no one among you wise enough to settle a dispute between the brothers" (1 Cor 6:5). Possibly a person whose gift is an utterance of wisdom would be best able to settle this kind of dispute.

In regard to those who are outside the church, believers are exhorted to act wisely. "Walk in wisdom toward outsiders, making the best use of the time. Let your speech always be gracious, seasoned with salt, so that you may know how you ought to answer each person" (Col 4:5–6). Acting wisely is connected here with speaking and answering. This suggests that wise words and wise answers are appropriate when dealing with people outside the church. This is a general command, given to all believers. However, I would expect that people whose gift is an utterance of wisdom would excel in their ability to speak wisely to unbelievers and would be able to answer difficult questions. This might be akin to what we would call apologetics. A word of wisdom could also be used to testify to the gospel in situations where there is persecution (see Luke 21:15).

As with other spiritual gifts there is a false or counterfeit wisdom. Paul warns the Colossians about falsely spiritual regulations. "These have indeed an appearance of wisdom in promoting self-made religion and asceticism and severity to the body, but they are of no value in stopping the indulgence of the flesh" (Col 2:23). The supposed spirituality which was fashionable in Colossae involved religious festival observance, boasting about visions, and worshipping angels (Col 2:16–18). These people were "not holding fast to the head," that is, to Jesus (Col 2:19). When wisdom is not centered on Jesus, then it is false wisdom. James also speaks of false wisdom, which manifests in jealousy and selfish ambition and boasting. "This is not the wisdom that comes down from above, but is earthly, unspiritual, demonic" (Jas 3:15). He contrasts this with godly wisdom. "But the wisdom from above is first pure, then peaceable, gentle, open to reason, full of mercy and good fruits, impartial and sincere" (Jas 3:17). The wisdom James speaks of involves some character qualities. It is not appropriate to compartmentalize the fruit of the Spirit and the gifts of the Spirit. There is one Spirit and he does not merely give one or the other but both. The use of the gifts of the Spirit is always within the context of a character shaped by the Holy Spirit. The Holy Spirit will always point us towards Jesus in both words and actions. If this is missing in an utterance of wisdom, then that gift is false.

The church needs people with the gift of utterance of wisdom. Words of wisdom from the Spirit can make the difference between being unable to decide what to do and confidently acting according to God's will. Each utterance of wisdom will apply the work of the cross to a situation or dilemma. It will point people to the glory of the crucified one, who is wisdom personified. Such utterances may seem strange because it is by weakness and not power that God transforms the world. However, the unique nature of the church requires that we live according to God's wisdom, and this gift can help make that possible.

15

Utterance of Knowledge

"For to one is given through the Spirit the utterance of wisdom, *and to another the utterance of knowledge according to
the same Spirit*" (1 Cor 12:8).

As WITH MANY OF the spiritual gifts mentioned in 1 Cor 12, there is no
explanation of what an utterance of knowledge actually entails. Some gifts
are easier to define because there is more description of them elsewhere.
An utterance of knowledge has been described, in the churches where I
have been involved, as a supernatural word from God about something
that would not otherwise be known. This is probably a reasonable description of the gift. However, supernatural knowledge is most likely a wider
category than simply knowing that someone in church has a particular
ailment. In order to understand this gift, I will consider instances of supernatural knowledge throughout the New Testament. The word "know"
is a common verb, but I am only concerned with supernatural knowledge.
By supernatural knowledge I mean knowledge that can only be gained by
revelation from God. This is usually given by the Holy Spirit.

In the Gospels, there are several examples of supernatural knowledge
that involve knowledge of God and the kingdom of God. I include this as
supernatural knowledge because not every person can know God and not
every person is able to understand the kingdom of God. John the Baptist
was appointed "to give knowledge of salvation to his people in the forgiveness of their sins" (Luke 1:77). This was part of his call to be a prophet who
made way for the Lord (Luke 1:76). When Jesus spoke to the crowds, he did

so in parables. The crowds did not understand what he was talking about, but Jesus explained his parables to his disciples, telling them, "To you it has been given to know the secrets of the kingdom of heaven, but to them it has not been given" (Matt 13:11). Like knowledge of salvation, knowledge of the kingdom of heaven is supernatural knowledge. It cannot be known unless it is revealed to us.

In many instances, Jesus had supernatural knowledge of events, what people were saying, what people were thinking, and also what was in people's hearts. There is no explicit explanation given for this supernatural knowledge. The general assumption that Jesus knew things because he is God is not a particularly helpful one when it comes to understanding the Christian life. Jesus is divine, but this has no parallel in the Christian experience. It seems more appropriate to understand Jesus' supernatural knowledge as the result of his anointing with the Holy Spirit at his baptism. Like the prophets of the Old Testament, Jesus knew things supernaturally because of the presence of the Holy Spirit within him. Jesus' anointing by the Spirit does find parallel in the Christian life since believers are similarly anointed by the Spirit.

There are many instances of supernatural knowledge in the life of Jesus. Jesus knew that the Pharisees were plotting to kill him (Matt 12:14–15). He knew that his disciples were talking behind his back about what he told them (Matt 16:7–8). He knew the evil intent of the hearts of those who came to ask him what seemed like a polite question (Matt 22:15–18). He knew about the private grumbling of his disciples (Matt 26:6–10). He knew that the chief priests had handed him over to Pilate out of envy (Mark 15:10). He knew that the woman with the uterine hemorrhage touched him (Luke 8:46). He had supernatural knowledge about Nathanael (John 1:48). He knew the hearts of people and therefore did not entrust himself to them (John 2:24–25). He knew the length of time that the crippled man had lain by the pool of Bethesda (John 5:6). He knew the spiritual condition of people around him (John 5:42). He knew that the crowds wanted to make him king by force (John 6:15).

There is another kind of supernatural knowledge that Jesus had, that is, knowledge of the Father. We need this knowledge to enter the kingdom of God. First of all, he alone knows the Father and is known by the Father. Yet he is willing to let others, those who he chooses, into this relationship (Luke 10:22; see also John 8:54–55). Jesus also has supernatural knowledge of his own sheep and gives them supernatural knowledge of him and of his voice (John 10:14, 27). Without supernatural knowledge, the Jews who saw Jesus, and even saw his miracles, did not know the relationship that Jesus had with the Father. Because they did not know this, they tried to stone him (John 10:38). Only those who are privileged to have the Holy Spirit indwelling them and to know him as the Spirit of truth can know the unique relationship between Jesus and the Father and can therefore be part of that relationship (John 14:17, 20).

Supernatural knowledge of God, given by Christ through his Spirit, is relational knowledge not knowledge of facts about God. If we disconnect relational supernatural knowledge from the spiritual gift, then we divorce the gift from the gospel. This results in all kinds of false ideas about how the gift is used and what it must look like. The substance of the gifts must be the gospel and the person of Christ. Without these, our understanding of gifts is overtaken by our cultural understandings of reality. In our culture, a gift is used for the benefit of the one who receives the gift. What I do with my gift is my business. I can use it or not, according to my choice. If I choose to use it, then I will do so for my own glory and my own advantage, and feel fully justified in doing so. This is what happens if the gifts of the Spirit are divorced from the gospel.

However, if we see the gifts of the Spirit as a means of proclaiming the gospel, then we will use the gifts for others that they might experience true knowledge of God through Jesus. Ultimately, every utterance of knowledge is intended to lead people to relational knowledge of God. An utterance of knowledge cannot simply be a matter of saying things unknown to the normal senses, as if the gifts of the Spirit were something akin to clairvoyance. Clairvoyants speak what seems like secret knowledge. They impress people with their ability to see these secret things. But this cannot be the way in which a believer uses an utterance of knowledge. Jesus knew all kinds of things that he would not naturally know. But these things were given to him to fulfill his mission of enabling other people to know God the Father as he knows the Father. He never simply said things in order to impress others with his capacity to see secrets to which no one else had access. An utterance of knowledge, then, must have a place in helping others (believers or unbelievers) to know the God who has revealed himself in the gospel. Utterances of knowledge may involve facts about people, events, thoughts, or motives of the heart, but these all are intended to lead to relational knowledge of God.

In the epistles, as with the Gospels, knowledge is frequently relational knowledge of God: knowledge of God (2 Cor 2:14); knowledge of the glory of God (2 Cor 4:6); knowledge of Christ (Phil 3:8; Col 2:2); and experiential knowledge of Christ's suffering and resurrection (Phil 3:10). All this knowledge is hidden in Christ (Col 2:3). Knowledge of God is not something natural (Rom 11:33–34), but only available through the Holy Spirit (1 Cor 2:11). An utterance of knowledge does not have to be directly about relational knowledge of God, but its purpose is still to lead to relational knowledge of God.

The gift of utterance of knowledge is found only in 1 Cor 12:8, so it is worth considering what this book can tell us about the gift. In Christ the Corinthians had been enriched in every way, in all speech (utterance) and all knowledge (1 Cor 1:5). It is interesting that this verse contains the combination of the Greek for "utterance" and "knowledge," and that it comes just prior to the statement that the Corinthians do not lack any spiritual gifts (1 Cor 1:7). This enrichment in speech (utterance) and knowledge is due to the confirmation of the testimony of Christ (1 Cor 1:6). This strongly implies that possession of spiritual gifts in general is a result of the church hearing and receiving the apostolic testimony of Christ, now encapsulated in the Bible. The more that Christ is proclaimed faithfully, truthfully, and fully, the more you would expect God to confirm this by the presence of spiritual gifts, and in particular an utterance of knowledge.

Sandwiched between the passages on spiritual gifts (1 Cor 12–14) is the famous chapter on love. Chapter 13 mentions knowledge four times (twice the noun and twice the verb). Given where these references to knowledge and knowing appear, these may tell us something about the gift of utterance of knowledge. In 1 Cor 13:2, knowledge appears along with other gifts, namely, prophecy and faith. Without love none of these gifts are of any value. In 1 Cor 13:8, knowledge is mentioned with two other gifts, that is, prophecy and tongues. These will all pass away "for we know in part and we prophesy in part" (1 Cor 13:9). Again knowing is put alongside a spiritual gift (prophecy). The utterance of knowledge, then, can only ever be partial. It is impossible to know everything about a situation or, more importantly, a person. To have an utterance of knowledge is not the same as reaching into the life of the person or the soul of the person and knowing everything about them. It is partial knowledge and partial knowing. It cannot be more since full knowledge of one another awaits the resurrection, just as full knowledge of God cannot be had right now. "For now we see in a mirror dimly, but then face to face. Now I know in part; then I shall know fully, even as I have been fully known" (1 Cor 13:12).

There are limits on what might constitute a valid utterance of knowledge. Paul warns Timothy against "the irreverent babble and contradictions of what is falsely called 'knowledge'" (1 Tim 6:20). Whatever he is referring to here, this makes plain that there are false kinds of knowledge, which should not be classed as knowledge by believers. The qualifiers here are "irreverent" and "contradiction." These are dangerous because some have wandered from the faith by embracing them (1 Tim 6:21). At minimum, this suggests the need to test any utterance claiming to be knowledge from the Holy Spirit. If it is contrary to the revealed faith about Jesus or in some way leads people away from Jesus, then it cannot be a genuine utterance from the Holy Spirit.

There are some things the Scripture declares we are definitely not able to know. Jesus told us that we cannot know the day or the hour when he will return. He does not even know this himself (Matt 24:36). We also are not given authority to know about times and seasons set by the Father's authority, such as when the kingdom will be restored to Israel (Acts 1:6–7). In addition, Jesus speaks of some who have not learned Satan's so-called deep secrets (Rev 2:24). These are not things Christians need to know. An utterance of knowledge should not claim to provide any knowledge not given for us to know. An utterance of knowledge has real boundaries. Outside those boundaries the gift is a false gift, not given by the Holy Spirit.

An utterance of knowledge can be a spectacular gift. However, its purpose is not to wow people but to point others to relational knowledge of God through Christ. It may reveal something unknown to the natural senses. But it will never venture into declarations of knowledge that believers are not given to know. The utterance of knowledge is not clairvoyance, but it is a practical outworking of God's love. It will manifest the gospel as it reveals what God knows about his people and that he knows them intimately.

16

Faith

"to another faith by the same Spirit" (1 Cor 12:9a).

FAITH IS AN EXCEPTIONALLY common word in the New Testament because of its importance to salvation. This makes understanding the gift of faith a little tricky in some respects. However, one kind of faith stands out as the gift of faith, believing the impossible to be possible.

In the New Testament, there are at least six different ways in which the word "faith" is used: faith in Jesus Christ or saving faith; "the faith," by which the Bible means the Christian faith; the measure of faith which is given to each person to operate gifts; faith that believes God answers prayer or trusts his promises; faithfulness as a fruit of the Spirit; and faith which moves mountains. Every Christian believer must have faith in Jesus Christ. Without this faith no one can be saved. This is not the gift of faith described in 1 Cor 12:9, but it is given as a gift of grace (Eph 2:8). Second, there is "the faith," the Christian faith as against the religion of Judaism (Acts 6:7; 13:8). We are also all instructed to keep the faith and stand firm in it, keeping to the revealed doctrines of the Christian faith and not deviating into false thinking. Being firm in the faith is staying in the path of life, continuing to be a follower of Jesus. This is also expected of every Christian. There is a measure of faith given to every Christian (Rom 12:3, 6) and this is what enables us to use the spiritual gifts we have been given for the kingdom of God. Prayer requires faith that God answers those who call on him (Heb 11:6). This is not the spiritual gift of faith either, although it given by grace. Faith is used in day to day life and trusts God's word (Rom 14:23). We live by faith and not by sight (2 Cor 5:7). Faithfulness is the same Greek word as faith. In Gal 5:22 it is listed as a fruit of the Spirit. Every believer is expected to grow in this. The final kind of faith described in the New Testament is the faith which moves mountains (1 Cor 13:13). This is not saving faith or belief in the truth of God's word but faith that trusts God so much that it believes impossible things will happen in response to prayer. I believe faith that moves mountains is the spiritual gift of faith.

Sometimes faith that believes God for the impossible coincides with saving faith. The centurion asked Jesus to heal his sick servant. But he would not let Jesus come to his house. He believed that Jesus could heal at a distance, even though up to that point in Matthew's Gospel Jesus had not done so. The centurion was commended as a man of great faith, greater than anyone in Israel (Matt 8:5–13). The faith of this Gentile resulted in an extraordinary miracle and his salvation (Matt 8:1–12). There is another person of great faith in Matthew, another Gentile, but this time a woman. The Canaanite woman exhibited great faith when she persisted in asking for her daughter's healing, even though Jesus first ignored her and then denied that she had any right to ask (Matt 15:21–28).

Jesus spoke of faith that moves mountains. When the disciples asked why they could not heal a demon-possessed boy, "He said to them, 'Because of your little faith. For truly, I say to you, if you have faith like a grain of mustard seed, you will say to this mountain, "Move from here to there," and it will move, and nothing will be impossible for you'" (Matt 17:20). On another occasion, "Jesus answered them, 'Truly, I say to you, if you have faith and do not doubt, you will not only do what has been done to the fig tree, but even if you say to this mountain, "Be taken up and thrown into the sea," it will happen'" (Matt 21:21). These examples of faith are not saving faith but faith that believes the impossible to happen.

Jesus demonstrated this kind of faith. In the case of the demon-possessed boy, he rebuked the demon and healed the boy (Matt 17:18). The context of the second saying was Jesus cursing the fig tree. "In the morning, as he was returning to the city, he became hungry. And seeing a fig tree by the wayside, he went to it and found nothing on it but only leaves. And he said to it, 'May no fruit ever come from you again!' And the fig tree withered at once" (Matt 21:18–19). What Jesus said happened immediately. He believed that the boy would be healed and he believed that the fig tree would be withered. This is the exercise of faith. There are some other examples of Jesus exercising faith. One day while Jesus was in a boat with his disciples, there was a great storm. Jesus was asleep, but the disciples were afraid that they would drown. Jesus calmed the storm and asked the disciples, "Why are you so afraid? Have you still no faith?" (Mark 4:35–40). Jesus calmed the storm by exercising faith. Faith on the part of Jesus is not mentioned in the case of other miracles. However, we might assume that Jesus had faith to do all the miraculous things he did.

There are some examples of the gift of faith in Acts. A crippled man at the Beautiful Gate was healed by the apostles. They tell the crowds, "And his name—by faith in his name—has made this man strong whom you see and know, and the faith that is through Jesus has given the man this perfect health in the presence of you all" (Acts 3:16). This miracle is an example of faith being exercised by the apostles in order to heal the sick. There is another example in Acts 14. "Now at Lystra there was a man sitting who could not use his feet. He was crippled from birth and had never walked. He listened to Paul speaking. And Paul, looking intently at him and seeing that he had faith to be made well, said in a loud voice, 'Stand upright on your feet.' And he sprang up and began walking" (Acts 14:8–10). It is not clear whether the man here had faith for salvation, and was subsequently healed of his disability, or whether he had faith to be healed, or both. But it is an example of faith connected to a miracle.

The faith mentioned in the epistles is mostly saving faith or "the faith." However, in 1 Cor 12, faith is mentioned as a gift of the Spirit: "to another faith by the same Spirit" (1 Cor 12:9a). In 1 Cor 13, Paul uses the word faith in two different ways. In 1 Cor 13:2, he speaks of faith that moves mountains. This seems to be the spiritual gift of faith since it is mentioned with another gift, prophecy. But in 1 Cor 13:13 he says that faith, hope, and love will remain. Since the gifts will pass away when the kingdom comes in its fullness (1 Cor 13:10), faith here cannot mean the spiritual gift, but rather saving faith.

Some people have more faith than do others. The famous faith chapter of Hebrews mentions some great heroes of faith. "Now faith is the assurance of things hoped for, the conviction of things not seen" (Heb 11:1). This may or may not be speaking about the gift of faith, but it is still a good definition of what that gift must look like. Those who exercise the gift of faith have a very strong assurance about what they do not see. They are sure that the thing will come to pass because that assurance is grounded in God and his gift to them. Some of the heroes of the faith include: Sarah, who was able to conceive because she believed God is faithful to his promises (Heb

11:11); Abraham, who by faith was willing to offer Isaac as a sacrifice because he believed that God raises the dead (Heb 11:17–19); and Isaac, who blessed his sons about their future by faith (Heb 11:20). Others "conquered kingdoms, enforced justice, obtained promises" and "stopped the mouths of lions" through faith (Heb 11:33). It is sometimes difficult to separate faith as a gift and faith as a character quality. However, these saints still exhibited faith and hence received the impossible as a result. I believe that the gift of faith is a gift of exceptional confidence that impossible things will happen.

In the epistle of James, there is an instruction for the sick. "Is anyone among you sick? Let him call for the elders of the church, and let them pray over him, anointing him with oil in the name of the Lord. And the prayer of faith will save the one who is sick, and the Lord will raise him up. And if he has committed sins, he will be forgiven" (Jas 5:14–15). This instruction presupposes that elders of the church will be able to offer a prayer for the sick with faith. Possibly faith is expected to be a character quality for elders. But it does connect faith to healing, paralleling what happens in the Gospels and Acts, where people are healed through faith. In my experience, not many elders of the church have successfully prayed for the sick. It is possible that those who prayed were gifted with faith in the time when James wrote. The prayer for the sick will be most effective if the elders who pray are those who have this gift.

Like the other gifts, faith can be exercised both inside the church and outside. Faith inside the church can be used when praying for God to do impossible things for his people. Outside the church it can be a demonstration of what God can do. It is related to healing the sick and doing miracles. It can also be used by those who must show themselves faithful to the Gospel in the light of persecution. There are many miraculous and impossible things God desires to do in the church and in the world. These will not happen without the exercise of faith. Therefore, many should pray to receive the gift of faith.

How is this gift connected to the gospel? People do not have faith in faith. Faith is always exercised in relation to the promises and character of God. Jesus is "the founder and perfecter of our faith" (Heb 12:2a). Although there are at least six understandings of faith in the New Testament, we can rightly say that Jesus is the founder and perfecter of them all. He is the first to trust God with an absolute trust. On the cross he believed the impossible. There were absolutely no indications of a future for Jesus while he was on the cross. He went into the grave with the dead. He appeared to be cut off from life and from the glorious presence of God. Yet Peter's Pentecost speech informs us that Jesus trusted in the word of God from Ps 16 regarding his resurrection—"therefore my heart was glad, and my tongue rejoiced; my flesh also will dwell in hope. For you will not abandon my soul to Hades, or let your Holy One see corruption" (Acts 2:26–27). Although he was dead and buried he believed he would be raised to glory. This was an exercise of the gift of faith. This faith in the face of no sign of God's goodness is the model for the gift of faith in others. Christians with faith can believe that God will honor his word even in the bleakest situation imaginable, when there is no outward sign that what is hoped for will happen.

God responds to prayers of faith. This is why the gift of faith is so important for the church. If his redemptive purposes are to be accomplished by his people, then the church needs to include people with the gift of faith. People with faith will ask God for the impossible and see it happen. This will edify the church and demonstrate to the world that Jesus Christ is lord over all.

17

Gifts of Healings

"to another gifts of healing by the one Spirit" (1 Cor 12:9b).

HEALINGS OCCUPY A LARGE part of the New Testament. People are restored to physical health and wholeness and also restored to relationship and to community inclusion. Healing is part of the kingdom of God that Jesus inaugurated when he came to earth. It points us toward a future state in which all will be fully healed by Jesus Christ.

In 1 Cor 12:8–10, some of the gifts are listed in singular form: utterance of wisdom, utterance of knowledge, faith, and the interpretation of tongues. But some are listed in plural form: gifts of healings, workings of miracles, distinguishings between spirits, and different kinds of tongues. These plurals do not necessarily come across well in the English translations, but they do suggest something about these particular gifts. Quite possibly the gifts in the plural lists have a variety of manifestations. So when a person speaks in tongues this involves speaking in different languages, rather than just one. Or possibly it means that each person with this gift speaks a different language. In the case of gifts of healings, there is another interesting aspect to note. It is the only one in the list with the word "gift" attached to it.

What might we conclude from the plural construction "gifts of healings"? There is no obvious grammatical reason for it, so it must have some other significance. Quite likely there are different kinds of healings implied here: physical healing, emotional healing, relational healing, or even spiritual healing. Since the gifts listed in 1 Cor 12:7–11 are (generally) preceded by "to another," including gifts of healings, it is reasonable to conclude that gifts of healings are given to one person, rather than different gifts of healing given to a group of people. In other words, those with gifts of healings are likely to be able to heal a variety of different things.

In the New Testament, there is more than one word used to mean healing. The particular word used in "gifts of healings" is *iama*. In the New Testament, the noun is only used in 1 Cor 12 (9, 28, 30), but the verb, *iaomai,* is used in many other places. It is frequently used in conjunction with other words for healing. *Iaomai* has a wider range of meaning than the other significant word for healing, *therapeuō*.

In the Septuagint (second-century BC Greek version of the Old Testament), *iaomai* is used in several different ways. It is not merely used of physical healing. Abimelech's wives were healed of their inability to have children (Gen 20:17) and Miriam was healed of leprosy (Num 12:13). In Deut 30:3, *iaomai* is used to mean *restore* the fortunes of Israel. Elijah healed a spring of water in 2 Kgs 2:21. Second Chronicles 7:14 promises that God will heal the land if the people of God turn to him, pray, and repent. In this case, healing is not bodily healing but healing of the land. In the Psalms, healing is of body and soul (Pss 6:2–4; 41:4; 147:3). Healing can involve restoration of relationship with God (Hos 6:1; 14:4; Isa 19:22). It includes restoration of peace (Isa 57:18) and healing of faithlessness (Jer 3:22).

In the New Testament, *iaomai* is generally used of physical healing but does have other nuances. I will examine the physical healings first. Jesus physically healed many people. The centurion's servant was healed at a distance (Matt 8:8, 13). The Canaanite's daughter was healed of her demon-possession (Matt 15:28). The woman with the uterine hemorrhage was healed of her bleeding (Mark 5:29). Luke 5:17 specifically mentions that "the power of the Lord was with him [Jesus] to heal." In this instance, the fact that Jesus was exercising a gift of healing is quite evident. On many occasions, large numbers of people were physically healed at one time (Luke 6:18; 9:11). Jesus healed people on the Sabbath (Luke 14:3–4) because freeing people from their infirmities is more important than following rules about rest. Jesus healed a number of other people, including one at the point of death (John 4:47) and a man who had been unable to walk for thirty-eight years (John 5:13). When one of the disciples cut an ear off the servant of the high priest who had come to arrest Jesus, Jesus healed the man (Luke 22:50–51). He healed even his enemies.

In several passages, *iaomai* is used side by side with *therapeuō*. In Luke 14:3–4, the two words for healing are used together, first *therapeuō* (v. 3) and then *iaomai* (v. 4). There seems to be no difference in meaning here. Other instances where these two words are used together are Matt 8:7–8, Luke 9:1–2, John 5:10, 13, and Acts 28:8–9. The different Gospel writers use different words for healing in their Gospels. The same story in a different Gospel can use *iaomai* in one and *therapeuō* in another (e.g., Luke 9:42 and Matt 17:16–18). Matthew uses *therapeuō* more often than Luke does and Luke uses *iaomai* more often than Matthew does, but they both use both words. Therefore, instances where *therapeuō* is used instead of *iaomai* might also shed light on the gifts of healings.

When *therapeuō* is used in the Gospels, it includes healing of sickness, pain, epilepsy, paralysis, the blind, the mute, the crippled, and those oppressed by demons (Matt 4:24; 15:30). Those possessed by demons are healed (Matt 17:16, 18). A demon-possessed man was blind and mute and healed by Jesus (Matt 12:22). In this case, physical healing and exorcism happen together. People were healed of their diseases and healed of unclean spirits (Luke 6:18) (both words are used here). Other people were healed of evil spirits and infirmities (Luke 7:21; 8:2). When the seventy-two were sent out, Jesus commanded them, "Heal the sick in it and say to them, 'The kingdom of God has come near to you'" (Luke 10:9), thereby connecting healing and the kingdom of God; healing is a sign that the kingdom has come (compare Matt 12:28). Many times Jesus healed on the Sabbath (Luke 13:14; 14:3; John 5:10). Therefore, healing makes sense in the context of the Sabbath. It points to God's eschatological Sabbath rest. Thus healing connects with salvation and the kingdom of God.

Healing can involve casting out demons (Matt 15:22, 28; Luke 9:42). People with unclean spirits are said to be healed (*therapeuō*) (Luke 6:18). Gifts sometimes overlap. In this case, healings may include exorcisms. If discerning between spirits involves being able to tell when demons are present, then the two gifts would need to work together in order for exorcisms to effectively take place.

Physical healing is connected with the gospel and the salvation of the person. In the story of the paralyzed man lowered through the roof to Jesus, the man was first forgiven and then healed (Luke 5:17–26). Luke 17:11–19 contains the story of ten lepers who begged Jesus to have mercy. They were cleansed of their ritual uncleanness. They were also healed. Only one came back to thank Jesus and he was told, "Your faith has made you well" (v.

19). "Made you well" translates the Greek word *sesōken*, which is frequently translated "saved." Only the man with faith has this said about him; faith in Christ brings salvation. When Jesus went to his home town he could not do any miracles or heal many because of their unbelief (Mark 6:5). Since his healings were so connected to the salvation he offered, he could do very few healings while they did not believe that he is Messiah. Because the healings of Jesus were connected to the kingdom of God, forgiveness, and salvation, we should expect the gifts of healings to point people to Jesus. The gifts of the Spirit are intended to be gospel-centered. They are all proclamations and demonstrations of the gospel in different ways.

In Acts, we find the same kinds of healings as are found in the Gospels. When the people realized that the apostles were healing the sick, many people came from around Jerusalem and were healed (Acts 5:16). The scene was repeated when Philip preached the gospel in Samaria (Acts 8:6–7). Peter went to see the church in Lydda and there healed a paralyzed man. The people of that place saw what had happened in the name of Jesus and many people believed in Jesus (Acts 9:32–35). In the next town, Peter raised a Christian woman from the dead. Again many people believed in Jesus as a result (Acts 9:36–42). When Paul was shipwrecked on Malta, he was looked after by Publius, the chief official of the island. While in his house, Paul healed Publius' father, who had dysentery and fever. Then every other sick person on the island came and was healed (Acts 28:7–9; this passage uses both words for healing). There is no indication of whether the people believed the gospel or not. Paul simply healed people because a need arose.

Healing the sick was a significant part of the witness of the early church to Jesus. After the apostles had been persecuted and released from prison, they prayed and asked God to grant them boldness, "while you stretch out your hand to heal, and signs and wonders are performed through the name of your holy servant Jesus" (Acts 4:30). When Peter preached his sermon about the gospel to Cornelius, he thought it important to include the fact that "God anointed Jesus of Nazareth with the Holy Spirit and with power. He went about doing good and healing all who were oppressed by the devil, for God was with him" (Acts 10:38). Clearly the fact that Jesus healed and cast out demons was important to the early church's witness. This fits well with what the apostles did in the name of Jesus—healing the sick and proclaiming the power of Jesus.

James instructs the sick person to call for the elders of the church to pray and anoint with oil (Jas 5:14–16). No mention is made of gifts of healings, which is a little surprising. Possibly, James assumes that one of the elders in the church would have a gift of healing. It is also possible that other gifts are expected to be used in this situation. "The prayer of faith will save the one who is sick" (v. 15) suggests that a gift of faith should operate here also. This passage connects physical healing and forgiveness, and also connects confession of sin with healing. Clearly a person who is sick has more needs than simply to be physically healed. People have need of other kinds of healing, including healing from sin and reconciliation with other people.

The word *iaomai,* which is frequently used of physical healing in the Gospels and Acts, is also used to mean healing that is not physical in nature, in accord with some of the Old Testament uses of the word. "For this people's heart has grown dull, and with their ears they can barely hear, and their eyes they have closed, lest they should see with their eyes and hear with their ears and understand with their heart and turn, and I would heal them" (Matt 13:15). This passage is a quotation from Isa 6:10. It is repeated in various forms in other places in the New Testament (John 12:40; Acts 28:26). The healing it refers to is healing from sin, from rejecting the God of Israel and allegiance to him. In the context of the New Testament, those who need to be healed are the people who refuse to believe that Jesus is the one come to save them and to usher in the kingdom of God. It is not physical healing that these people need. Rather they need to be healed of their rebellion and sinfulness. They need healing so that they are able to respond to the gospel, a healing which enables faith. This is consistent with the other passages where physical healing is connected to the salvation of the person.

Once in the Gospels Jesus calls himself a doctor (*iatros*—a word connected to *iaomai*). He said, "Those who are well have no need of a physician, but those who are sick. I came not to call the righteous, but sinners" (Mark 2:17; see also Matt 9:12; Luke 5:31). Jesus does not mean here that he is a doctor who heals the body but rather one who heals the affliction of sin. Sinners came to him because he offered them forgiveness and acceptance. People recognized that Jesus came to bring salvation to his people. In this instance, Doctor Jesus heals people from sin, not diseases, sickness, or bodily weakness.

Other uses of the word *iaomai* for non-physical healing are found in the New Testament. The first is in Heb 12:13. In this passage, healing refers to enabling people who have been undergoing suffering to persevere in the trial, knowing that they are under the discipline of a loving God. Physical healing is definitely not in view. The next passage is frequently quoted by some Pentecostals. "He himself bore our sins in his body on the tree, that we might die to sin and live to righteousness. By his wounds you have been healed. For you were straying like sheep, but have now returned to the Shepherd and Overseer of your souls" (1 Pet 2:24–25). Verse 24 is often used to "prove" that we need only to claim our healing since we have been healed by the stripes of Jesus. However, the context tells a different story. The healing provided by the stripes of Jesus is healing from sin. Now that we have been healed because of the cross, we can live in righteousness and be reconciled to God, instead of living like sinners who are in rebellion against him. This is not speaking of physical healing.

The final mention of healing in the Bible is in Rev 22:1–2. "Then the angel showed me the river of the water of life, bright as crystal, flowing from the throne of God and of the Lamb through the middle of the street of the city; also, on either side of the river, the tree of life with its twelve kinds of fruit, yielding its fruit each month. The leaves of the tree were for the healing of the nations." The nations will be completely healed by the water of life. This is a picture of the perfect peace (*shalom*) which will be present in the New Heavens and the New Earth. There will be reconciliation, peace, joy, integration of the different people of God, and no more curse. All who dwell there will know God and share in his life. None of the consequences of sin will exist in that place. The healings of the New Testament point towards this final state of humanity. Although most of the healings mentioned in the New Testament are physical, there are other nuances to healing and each one will find its completion in the city of God.

There is also a false gift of healing. In the book of Revelation, the first beast was healed of a mortal wound (Rev 13:3–4). Consequently the inhabitants of the earth (in contrast with those whose home is in heaven) follow the beast instead of following Jesus. Like false signs and wonders, false healings serve to lead people away from God, allow them to believe what suits them, and to shore up their idol worship (see 2 Thess 2:11). Where true gifts of the Spirit exist, the false will likely exist. We must not assume that because something appears supernatural that it must be the work of the Holy Spirit. The Holy Spirit will always point us to Jesus and give glory to him. False gifts will give glory elsewhere.

Healings in the New Testament are mainly physical, but they do include relational and spiritual healing. Those with gifts of healings, then, are able to provide different kinds of healing. Healing must point people to Jesus, who offers salvation of the whole person. Because this is a manifestly supernatural gift, it must always be accompanied by proclamation of the gospel. Without this, people may be awed by the power of the healing and lose sight of who gave it.

18

Working of Miracles

"to another the working of miracles" (1 Cor 12:10a).

WORKING OF MIRACLES IS another of the manifestly supernatural gifts. For this reason, we must be careful to consider how to use it wisely in order to give Jesus glory. It is important not to become enamored of raw power without the gospel of grace. God desires a mature use of this gift in his church.

The phrase "working (*energēma*) of miracles (*dynamis*)" implies an action rather than someone who prays for the miraculous to happen. The noun *energēma* is uncommon, but the verb *energeō* appears many times the New Testament. The two words *energeō* and *dynamis* appear together several times. In Gal 3:5, there is a similar expression to "the working of miracles" (found in 1 Cor 12:10). "Does he who supplies the Spirit to you and works miracles among you do so by works of the law, or by hearing with faith"? (Gal 3:5). The combination also appears in the Gospels. King Herod heard about Jesus and thought that he must be John the Baptist come back from the dead. "That is why these miraculous powers are at work in him" (Matt 14:1–2; Mark 6:14). In these passages, *dynamis* clearly means miracle. However, when the words appear together elsewhere, miracles do not seem to be in mind. "Now to him who is able to do far more abundantly than all that we ask or think, according to the power (*dynamis*) at work (*energeō*) within us," (Eph 3:20). Here the power of God is not doing miracles on the outside of the person but rather on the inside, changing us into Christ-like people. "For this I toil, struggling with all his energy that he powerfully works within me" (Col 1:29). The power at work in Paul was power to proclaim the gospel and to bring the church to maturity.

The working of miracles is intrinsically connected with the resurrection of Jesus. Ephesians 1:19–20 tells us of "the immeasurable greatness of his [God's] power toward us who believe, according to the working of his great might that he worked in Christ when he raised him from the dead and seated him at his right hand in the heavenly places." The Gospel accounts also link the miracles of Jesus to his resurrection. They do so by using the word *egeirō*, which means "wake up," "raise up," or "raise the dead." In secular Greek, it is used in all these ways but not of healing the sick. But the Gospel writers often use *egeirō* in stories about the sick being healed. When a paralyzed man was brought to Jesus to be healed, Jesus said, "'For which is easier, to say, "Your sins are forgiven," or to say, "Rise (*egeirō*) and walk"? But that you may know that the Son of Man has authority on earth to forgive sins'—he then said to the paralytic—"Rise (*egeirō*), pick up your mat and go home." And he rose (*egeirō*) and went home" (Matt 9:5–7; see also 9:25 and 17:7). The connection to the resurrection becomes clear when we observe that *egeirō* is repeatedly used to speak of Jesus being raised from the dead (Matt 16:21; 17:9, 23; 20:19; 26:32; 27:63–64; 28:6–7).

The preaching of the apostles in Acts also links the power of miracles to the resurrection of Jesus. After a crippled man had been healed at the temple, Peter told the people there, "Men of Israel, why do you wonder at this, or why do you stare at us, as though by our own power or piety we have made him walk? . . . you killed the Author of life, whom God raised from the dead" (Acts 3:12, 15a). The connection between power and the resurrection appears again in Acts 4:33a. "And with great power the apostles were giving their testimony to the resurrection of the Lord Jesus." This is consistent with the fact that whenever there was a miraculous event the apostles or deacons testified to Jesus (e.g., Acts 6:8–10; 8:4–8). Working of miracles, as with the other gifts of the Spirit, is intended to help proclaim the gospel of Jesus Christ. It cannot stand alone as some kind of spectacle without the substance of the gospel that Jesus died for our sins and was raised again from the dead.

There is a danger in seeing the working of miracles as a proof of godliness. Jesus warned, "Not everyone who says to me, 'Lord, Lord,' will enter the kingdom of heaven, but the one who does the will of my Father who is in heaven. On that day many will say to me, 'Lord, Lord, did we not prophesy in your name, and cast out demons in your name, and do many mighty works in your name?' And then I will declare to them, 'I never knew you; depart from me, you workers of lawlessness'" (Matt 7:21–23). The capacity to work miracles does not mean that a person will necessarily do the will of God or even that the person will give glory to Jesus in working the miracle. It is by no means a demonstration of godliness.

This danger might apply to other gifts as well. The gifts of the Spirit are not a sign of maturity, but simply gifts. We might make an analogy with the capacity of a sixteen-year-old to own a car. Ownership of a car does not make a good driver. Becoming a mature Christian, who obeys the will of God and gives glory to Jesus, must be worked on independently of possessing a particular gift. The person must practice obedience and spiritual disciplines. When maturity is not evident in the life of the person, the possession of a spectacular gift may lead to pride or arrogance. Others may become envious. Envy of other people's gifts is a sign of immaturity as well. Because there are real dangers in being thrill-seekers after the miraculous, the church needs maturity in order to handle the gift of working of miracles.

There are some people who teach that if the church were able to perform more miracles this would aid evangelism. Miracles and wonders were given to confirm the message of the gospel (Mark 16:20; Acts 14:3). The fact that God performed signs and wonders among the Gentiles was also used as proof that God desired Gentiles as part of the church (Acts 15:12). Paul includes the working of signs and wonders as part of his gospel proclamation to the Gentiles (Rom 15:18–19). God has testified to the gospel through signs, wonders, and miracles (Heb 2:4). The working of miracles must come from the Holy Spirit and lead to testimony about Jesus. The goal of the miraculous is to bring people to faith in Christ.

Although miracles may sometimes aid evangelism, they do not guarantee that people will be converted or that they will become true disciples of Jesus. Paul and Barnabas performed many signs and wonders among the Jews in Iconium (Acts 14:3). "But the people of the city were divided; some sided with the Jews and some with the apostles. When an attempt was made by both Gentiles and Jews, with their rulers, to mistreat them and to stone them" (Acts 14:4–5). The miraculous did not necessarily result in converts, let alone true disciples. Indeed, miracles will sometimes stand as evidence against people on the day of judgment because those who see miracles refuse to repent and believe in Jesus Christ (see Matt 11:20–23).

No one is surprised by the statement that Jesus did miracles, but we should not think that his miraculous power was drawn from his divinity.

Instead, he ministered in the power of the Holy Spirit. Since Jesus derived his power to do miracles from the Holy Spirit, he was able to pass on this ministry to others. He gave power to his twelve disciples to cast out demons and to heal the sick (Luke 9:1). This was an extension of his ministry. The miraculous continued in the book of Acts. The apostles are credited with many miracles early in Acts, but later others also did miracles. Philip did miracles in Samaria (Acts 8:6–7, 13). Philip was able to do these because he was a man full of the Holy Spirit (Acts 6:3, 5). The capacity to do miracles does not follow from being appointed to an office in the church, but it is given by the Holy Spirit.

There were levels of the miraculous done by different people. "And God was doing extraordinary miracles by the hands of Paul, so that even handkerchiefs or aprons that had touched his skin were carried away to the sick, and their diseases left them and the evil spirits came out of them" (Acts 19:11–12). Paul did not even have to be present for miracles to happen. There are other extraordinary miracles in Acts. People brought the sick out into the street and some were healed as Peter's shadow fell on them (Acts 5:15). The fact that some miracles in the Gospels and in Acts are more amazing than others has implications for the gift of working miracles. Some miracles will be small and some great. The gift may grow more powerful with use. Some people with the gift may have it in greater measure than do others (in accordance with the grace of God given to the person— Rom 12:6). The point is that the person who exercises the gift should not be judged according to the extent of the miracles. Nor should the person judge himself or herself on this basis. What matters is that the gift should be exercised in faith and according to the grace of God.

"And God was doing extraordinary miracles by the hands of Paul" (Acts 19:11) implies that the gift of working miracles involves people. God does not work without using people. That is why he has given the church a variety of spiritual gifts. If we do not seek and exercise the gifts, then the work of God will not be done in the world. God will not simply take over the task and do it for us. Instead, he equips his church and sends them out to do his work, including doing miraculous things. There is a lack of miraculous happenings in the western church. It is therefore time to earnestly seek spiritual gifts. I am not saying that we must each seek to be workers of miracles. This is something determined by the Holy Spirit. I say only that we should seek to embrace the gifts of the Spirit so that some people will receive the gift of working miracles. The general denigration or simple ignorance about the gifts of the Spirit means that many people don't even consider these important in the Christian life.

Miracles appear to overlap somewhat with healing and exorcism since these are included in the powerful things (*dynamis*) that Jesus did (e.g., Mark 5:30; 9:38–39; Luke 4:36; 5:17; 6:19). However, Jesus did many miracles that are neither healings nor exorcisms. Jesus walked on water and enabled Peter to also walk on water (Matt 14:25–29). He fed five thousand men and then four thousand men plus women and children (Matt 14:13–21; 15:29–38). He told Peter to go fishing in order to find a coin to pay the temple tax (Matt 17:27). Jesus calmed the storm with a word (Matt 8:23–27). He raised several people from the dead: a twelve-year-old girl (Mark 5:35–43); the son of a widow (Luke 7:11–17); and Lazarus (John 11). At the wedding in Cana Jesus turned water into wine (John 2:1–11).

In Acts, we also find miracles that are not healings. Ananias and Sapphira died because they lied to the Holy Spirit (Acts 5:1–11). This might or might not be understood as a miracle, but it was definitely a supernatural event. Peter raised Dorcas from the dead (Acts 9:36–41). Peter's escape from prison was the result of the prayers of the church (Acts 12:1–19). This may be an example of working of miracles. Paul told Elymas that he would be blind for a time because he opposed the gospel (Acts 13:9–11). Paul and Barnabas were supernaturally released from prison (Acts 16:25–28). Paul raised Eutychus from the dead at Troas (Acts 20:7–12). Paul was miraculously spared, along with all who were with him, when the ship he was on was shipwrecked (Acts 27:27–44). Some of these miracles were the result of prayer and some were spontaneous moves of the Holy Spirit. We should not limit the ways in which miracles take place. Some of these were miraculous judgments on people. This might be compared to the plagues that came upon Egypt through Moses.

The gospel is the power (*dynamis*) of God for the salvation of those who believe in Jesus Christ (Rom 1:16). Without the gospel any miraculous (*dynamis*) acts would be meaningless and evil. God's power is demonstrated in his act of love towards us in the cross (1 Cor 1:18). There Jesus was weak, and this weakness is the power of God. The true miracle will point towards the cross. It will not be an act of raw power. God is not a god of raw power but a God who displays his power in the weakness of the cross. Any act of raw power will be impressive to our thinking, but it is not from God. Since there are false miracles done through the power of the devil (see below), we must be discerning.

In keeping with the fact that God's power is demonstrated in the cross, we find the power of God among believers as they meet together in the name of Jesus (1 Cor 5:4), and among those who are persecuted and who endure great hardship for Jesus' sake (2 Cor 6:3–10). His power is made perfect in weakness (2 Cor 12:9). Those who wish to demonstrate the power of God must endure weakness. Therefore, people who exercise the gift of working of miracles must experience weakness. This idea is certainly backed up by the experience of the apostles in Acts. They proclaimed Christ, did miracles, and were often arrested and beaten. Some were killed.

There is a false gift of miracles. Jesus warned us, "false christs and false prophets will arise and perform great signs and wonders, so as to lead astray, if possible, even the elect" (Matt 24:24). Simon practiced magic in Samaria and people called him "the power of God that is called Great" since he astounded people with his magic (Act 8:9–11). These kinds of false miracles are the devil (or Satan) at work, trying to lead people away from the truth. Indeed, this is to be expected, because when the antichrist arises, he will do amazing signs and wonders. "The coming of the lawless one is by the activity of Satan with all power and false signs and wonders, and with all wicked deception for those who are perishing, because they refused to love the truth and so be saved. Therefore God sends them a strong delusion, so that they may believe what is false" (2 Thess 2:9–11). People who will believe these false miracles have been given over to believe lies instead of the truth. For this reason, godly Christians need to be aware and wary about miracles. How do we tell which are real and which are false miracles? The most significant test is to ask to whom the glory goes. If the glory goes to the person performing the miracle, then it is false. If the glory goes to Jesus, then it is a true miracle.

Working of miracles is a gift that is rare in the western church, but it is needed. God desires to act powerfully among his people. In performing miracles, the church points to the resurrection of Jesus and is enabled to proclaim the gospel with the power of the Holy Spirit. Miracles may take many forms, such as healings, deliverance from prison, exorcism, power over the elements, or raising the dead. Whatever kind of miracle is performed, this must be done in the name of Jesus and accompanied by gospel proclamation. Anything with does not glorify Jesus is a false miracle.

19

Distinguishing between Spirits

"to another the ability to distinguish between spirits"
(1 Cor 12:10c).

THERE IS MORE THAN one possibility for what the gift of distinguishing between spirits involves. It may be about knowing whether a prophecy is true or false, discerning true or false uses of spiritual gifts in general, discerning the presence of demons in a person, discerning when the Holy Spirit is operating, seeing angels, or knowing what is in the heart of a person.

One possibility is that this gift involves being able to tell if a prophetic word is from the Holy Spirit or not. This idea derives from the statement "Let two or three prophets speak, and let the others *weigh* what is said" (1 Cor 14:29). This is probably too narrow an understanding of the gift. Also, prophets are more likely to be the ones to discern whether prophecy is legitimate or not. Another possibility is that the gift involves discerning the use of all the gifts, not simply prophecy. This is suggested by the way in which "spirits" is used in 1 Cor 14:12—"So with yourselves, since you are eager for manifestations of the Spirit, strive to excel in building up the church." The ESV translates the word "spirits" here as "manifestations of the Spirit." The NIV translates it as "gifts of the Spirit." Either way, "spirits" is being used to describe what the church does with the gifts of the Spirit. If distinguishing between spirits includes being able to tell whether a particular gift is a manifestation of the Holy Spirit and not a manifestation of the flesh or a counterfeit gift, then this would be very helpful to the church.

There is another possibility. Distinguishing between spirits may involve being able to perceive spiritual activity and determine whether it is the Holy Spirit, the human spirit, or a demonic spirit which is active. It is necessary for all people to discern matters of a spiritual nature. Jesus told the Pharisees and Sadducees, "You know how to *interpret* the appearance of the sky, but you cannot *interpret* the signs of the times" (Matt 16:3). If they had been people who distinguished between spirits, they would have known that they were speaking to the Messiah. Instead, they rejected Jesus, to their own spiritual doom.

Casting out demons or unclean spirits presupposes that the person is able to discern the presence and possibly the number of unclean spirits. In the Gospels and in Acts, there are large numbers of exorcisms. Not only did Jesus cast out demons (e.g., Matt 8:16; Mark 9:25), but he gave the twelve authority over unclean spirits as well (Matt 10:1). In the Gospels, we find that many people brought their demon-possessed friends and relatives to Jesus. "But immediately a woman whose little daughter had an unclean spirit heard of him and came and fell down at his feet" (Mark 7:25). The woman was aware that the problem her daughter had was the result of a demon. Other people in the Gospels seem to have had no trouble seeing demonic possession. It did not appear to require a gift of distinguishing between spirits in order for them to perceive the presence of demons. But, by the same token, it is clear that they did not always get it right, because some people accused Jesus of having a demon (Mark 3:30). There was a distinctly different worldview at the time of Jesus. In our culture, we are unlikely to be able to perceive demons so easily. The gift of distinguishing between spirits is thus very important.

But distinguishing between spirits is not merely about discerning the demonic. It also involves being able to perceive the presence of the Holy Spirit. The Pharisees accused Jesus of casting out demons by Beelzebul, the prince of demons (Matt 12:24) and Jesus responded, "But if it is by the Spirit of God that I cast out demons, then the kingdom of God has come upon you" (Matt 12:28). The Pharisees were unable to discern the work of the Holy Spirit; their eyes were blind to him. On the other hand, Simeon recognized the infant Jesus through the Holy Spirit. Simeon was a righteous man who was waiting for the consolation of Israel. The Holy Spirit revealed to him that he would see the Messiah before he died. So when he saw Mary and Joseph with the infant Jesus in the temple, he knew by the Holy Spirit that the infant was the Messiah (Luke 2:25–32). Simeon correctly distinguished between spirits by the power of the Holy Spirit. In this, he was the complete opposite of the Pharisees who accused Jesus of being demon-possessed.

Distinguishing between spirits may include the ability to perceive the nature of the heart. The heart is the source of evil behavior (Matt 15:19). Jesus often discerned the thoughts of people's hearts. The teachers of the law thought it blasphemous that Jesus forgave sins. He said to them, "Why do you think evil in your hearts?" (Matt 9:4). The Pharisees sent people to trap Jesus in his words. They flattered him saying, "Teacher, we know that you are true and teach the way of God truthfully." But Jesus saw straight through them (Matt 22:16–18). He knew that he would be betrayed. When Judas asked him, "Is it I, Rabbi?" Jesus replied, "You have said so" (Matt 26:25). These may also be examples of an utterance of knowledge or they may involve distinguishing between spirits. Possibly the two gifts overlap here.

Peter discerned the heart of Ananias and Sapphira. The husband and wife lied about the money they got for selling their property. "But Peter said, 'Ananias, why has Satan filled your heart to lie to the Holy Spirit and to keep back for yourself part of the proceeds of the land?" (Acts 5:3). Peter discerned what was actually motivating Ananias. He saw beyond the surface and knew the intentions of the heart. Another instance of discernment is found in Acts 8. Simon the sorcerer believed the preaching of Philip and was baptized (v. 13). But when he saw how people received the Holy Spirit by the laying on of the apostles' hands, he tried to buy this power (vv. 18–19). Peter discerned that his heart was not right before God and called him to repentance (vv. 20–23). The gift also operated in Paul. Paul discerned that the slave girl who was following him and his companions had a spirit of divination. She was saying, "These men are servants of the Most High God, who proclaim to you the way of salvation" (Acts 16:17). This truthful statement did not prevent Paul from seeing the evil spirit at work in her.

The church needs to distinguish between spirits because without this gift we are open to all kinds of distortions of the gospel, spoken by false prophets and false apostles. "Beware of false prophets, who come to you in sheep's clothing but inwardly are ravenous wolves" (Matt 7:15). False apostles come into the church, claiming to be workers for Jesus, for "even Satan disguises himself as an angel of light" (2 Cor 11:13–14). Since the outward appearance of these people is no indication of what is inside, many people may be deceived and led astray from the truth and from relationship with God if no one discerns what is actually going on. It is clear that this deception has been going on for two thousand years. Paul observes, "For if someone comes and proclaims another Jesus than the one we proclaimed, or if you receive a different spirit from the one you received, or if you accept a different gospel from the one you accepted, you put up with it readily enough" (2 Cor 11:4).

The antichrist and the beast of Revelation come across to the world as charismatic men (or women) who are worth following. If this were not the case, then why would anyone follow these evil people? They will even do miracles (Rev 13:13) and deceive people. Jesus warned that false christs and false prophets will deceive even the elect (Matt 24:24). The gift of distinguishing between spirits can play a positive role in exposing evil people who appear on the outside to be worthy but underneath are against Christ and against his people.

Some matters are easier to discern than are others. For people with a gift of teaching, or even for people who regularly study the Bible, it can be easy to spot when someone teaches a false doctrine. However, when there is nothing obviously false being said, discerning the false prophet is more difficult. The nature of falsehood is that it is generally wrapped in a coating of truth. Those who distinguish between spirits are able to cut through the wrappings and façade and see what is going on underneath. They can see the motivations of people's hearts. The wolves, the false apostles, and the ones masquerading as believers need to be uncovered. It is the person who distinguishes between spirits who we need in this situation.

The manifestations of demons may be overt in a person, but so often they are not. The devil is called "the prince of the power of the air." He is at work in all those who do not obey the gospel of Christ (Eph 2:2). There is a pervasive brainwashing in culture, which makes the actions of people around us seem ordinary and acceptable. Yet the devil is at work in each one of them. Since this is so subtle, it can be easy to get sucked into thinking that everything is normal and appropriate. Those who distinguish between spirits will see through the ordinary and clearly see the work of the evil one. On the other hand, they will also be able to see what the Holy Spirit is doing in unbelievers.

There is another kind of spirit, other than the human spirit, the Holy Spirit, and demonic spirits, which is present in the world—angels. Angels are "ministering spirits sent out to serve for the sake of those who are to inherit salvation" (Heb 1:14). Angels are at work all the time, ministering to

Christians everywhere. This is not obvious in the natural realm. But Christians with the gift of distinguishing between spirits may be able to see what angels are doing and make that known to the rest of the church. This would encourage believers. We have real need of this kind of encouragement since it will remind us that God has not left us without help in times of difficulty.

People who can distinguish between spirits are able to perceive much that other Christians cannot. They are able to distinguish between the human spirit, the Holy Spirit, demonic spirits, and angels. They can discern the motivations of the heart. Distinguishing between spirits is a gift the church needs in order to cut through the false and find what is true.

20

Tongues and Interpretation of Tongues

"to another various kinds of tongues, to another the interpretation of tongues" (1 Cor 12:10d).

ALTHOUGH VARIOUS KINDS OF tongues and the interpretation of tongues are distinct gifts, they are integrally connected to one another. The latter can only be used when the former is exercised. The former is best used in congregational settings when the latter is available. Therefore, I will consider these together.

One significant way in which speaking in tongues is different from other gifts is that it cannot be understood by looking at the life of Jesus directly since there is no indication in the Gospels that Jesus ever prayed in tongues. The content of Jesus' personal prayer life is mentioned sparsely in the Gospels. The Gospels tell us that Jesus prayed, but often not what or how he prayed. Of the prayers Jesus prayed in public and examples he gave for his disciples to follow, none were prayed in languages foreign to the hearers.

Did Jesus pray in tongues then? We can only speculate about this. If it is a gift for private use, except if interpretation is given (this will be discussed later), then there would be no eye witnesses to such an activity in the life of Jesus. Since the gifts of the Spirit were not widely operative in other people during Jesus' lifetime, who could have interpreted his proclamations in tongues to the crowds? Only Jesus himself could have done this. But there was no purpose in this because he was clearly a prophet and spoke intelligible words that required no interpretation. However, since the gifts of the Holy Spirit must find their basis in the person of Jesus and his relationship with the Holy Spirit, it seems most likely that Jesus did pray in tongues in private.

There is a problem with the human tongue. What people say and how they use the tongue indicates what is in the heart. "For out of the abundance of the heart the mouth speaks" (Matt 12:34). Human sin makes human words often hurtful and evil. The human heart before regeneration is "deceitful above all things, and desperately sick" (Jer 17:9). As a consequence, David says of the wicked, who rebel against God, "there is no truth in their mouth; their inmost self is destruction; their throat is an open grave; they flatter with their tongue" (Ps 5:9). Paul repeats this Psalm in Rom 3:13. The wicked person has a mouth "filled with cursing and deceit and oppression" (Ps 10:7). It is very hard to tame the tongue. "And the tongue is a fire, a world of unrighteousness. The tongue is set among our members, staining the whole body, setting on fire the entire course of life, and set on fire by hell" (Jas 3:6). Peter offers a similar reminder. "Whoever desires to love life and see good days, let him keep his tongue from evil and his lips from speaking deceit" (1 Pet 3:10).

The tongue should be used to speak well of those made in the image of God. It is intended to proclaim the goodness of God and to utter his praise (Ps 35:28). God promised that all the nations would call upon the name of the LORD (Zeph 3:9). Every tongue will ultimately confess that Jesus is Lord (Phil 2:11). This is the purpose of the tongue. But since the tongue does not naturally praise God, how can we do what is right with the tongue? The answer is that the tongue is tamed by the Holy Spirit. "Therefore I want you to understand that no one speaking in the Spirit of God ever says 'Jesus is accursed!' and no one can say 'Jesus is Lord' except in the Holy Spirit" (1 Cor 12:3). The gift of speaking in tongues enables the tongue to be tamed, at least briefly. While the person is speaking in tongues through the Holy Spirit, there can be no cursing, no lying, and no utterance of evil.

The New Testament discussion of this gift is concentrated in the book of Acts and in 1 Cor 12–14. But before discussing these we must consider what is said in Mark's Gospel regarding tongues. Jesus said, "And these signs will accompany those who believe: in my name they will cast out demons; they will speak in new tongues; they will pick up serpents with their hands; and if they drink any deadly poison, it will not hurt them; they will lay their hands on the sick, and they will recover" (Mark 16:17–18). Some issues surround this passage. Most Bibles note that the earliest manuscripts of Mark's

Gospel do not contain the verses after 16:8. Therefore, there is a question about the authenticity of this saying of Jesus. From my perspective, it seems odd that Mark would have ended his Gospel at 16:8, so it is not strange that someone has put in this ending. But there is real uncertainty about whether to consider these verses inspired Scripture.

Many conservative evangelicals do not believe that sign gifts operate in the church anymore, so they are content to dismiss this passage on that ground as well. There is, however, no biblical warrant for dismissing the gifts mentioned in Mark 16:17 as if they had ceased to operate. The real issue is whether this passage says that *every* Christian will be able to cast out demons, speak in tongues, pick up snakes, and heal the sick. At first glance it seems so. However, let us consider the change between 16:15–16 and 16:17–18. "And [Jesus] said to them, 'Go into all the world and proclaim the gospel to the whole creation. Whoever believes and is baptized will be saved, but whoever does not believe will be condemned" (vv. 15–16). Notice how verse 16 is speaking about an individual who believes and an individual who does not believe. The salvation of an individual requires a personal decision to believe in Jesus Christ. But in verses 17–18, the focus changes away from individuals to a group, *those* who believe. Now the statements are not about individuals but about the church as a whole. In the church, these gifts will be operating. There will be those who cast out demons, those who speak in tongues, those who pick up snakes, and those who heal the sick. So the passage is not saying that *every* individual Christian will do each of these things. But it is saying that within the wider church there will be people who do.

The book of Acts contains actual examples of people speaking in tongues on the day of Pentecost. The believers were gathered together in Jerusalem, praying for the gift of God, the Holy Spirit, to be sent from heaven as Jesus had promised them (Acts 1:4–5, 14). The Holy Spirit was poured out in spectacular fashion, with a powerful wind and tongues of flame.

> And they were all filled with the Holy Spirit and began to speak in other tongues as the Spirit gave them utterance. Now there were dwelling in Jerusalem Jews, devout men from every nation under heaven. And at this sound the multitude came together, and they were bewildered, because each one was hearing them speak in his own language. And they were amazed and astonished, saying, 'Are not all these who are speaking Galileans? And how is it that we hear, each of us in his own native language?' . . . —we hear them

telling in our own tongues the mighty works of God' (Acts 2:4–8, 11b).

The early Christians all exercised the spiritual gift of speaking in tongues on that day.

The passage tells us some important things about this gift. First, the Christians actually spoke intelligible languages. We know this because the Diaspora Jews—those who had come to Jerusalem for Pentecost from various different countries—could understand what was being said. It was spoken in their own languages. Paul's mention of the tongues of humans and tongues of angels (1 Cor 13:1) also suggests that the gift of speaking in tongues involves speech that is intelligible to someone, either in the world or among angels. It is important to remember this since some have claimed that speaking in tongues is nothing more than gibberish brought out of the inner being of the speaker. Unless there is a native speaker of that particular language present, it is unlikely that the tongue will be understood, but this does not mean that the genuine gift is meaningless.

Second, the people who heard the tongues said, "we hear them telling in our own tongues the mighty works of God" (Acts 2:11). The purpose of speaking in tongues was the proclamation of the gospel. The believers on the day of Pentecost did not speak in tongues simply to act out a miracle or to do something supernatural. They did so because in this way God proclaimed the gospel to the people present. He demonstrated that the promise he had made through Joel (2:28–32) was fulfilled because of Jesus, who is the Messiah. Therefore, speaking in tongues is solidly connected to the gospel.

There are other instances in Acts where people spoke in tongues. The first is in Acts 10. Up to this point the apostles had only proclaimed the gospel to Jews and Samaritans (who were half-Jewish and who were familiar with the Scriptures). But in Acts 10 something new took place. Peter was given a vision and told to go to a Gentile, who was told by an angel to send for Peter. These things were necessary in order to get the gospel to the Gentiles since no Jew would set foot in a Gentile house. Peter proclaimed the gospel to the household of Cornelius. He did not actually expect what happened. "While Peter was still saying these things, the Holy Spirit fell on all who heard the word. And the believers from among the circumcised who had come with Peter were amazed, because the gift of the Holy Spirit was poured out even on the Gentiles. For they were hearing them speaking in tongues and extolling God. Then Peter declared, 'Can anyone withhold water for baptizing these people, who have received the Holy Spirit just as we have?'" (Acts 10:44–47).

In this case, speaking in tongues and praising God were signs of the outpouring of the Holy Spirit. Here the gift was not directed at people who spoke different languages, as was the case in Acts 2. No one understood what was being said. But the hearers did understand that the Holy Spirit had been poured out on the Gentiles. Without this sign, there would have been no assurance for Peter that the Gentiles could also be saved. In the light of this evidence, he found that he could not deny what God had done, so he ordered that they be baptized in water (Acts 10:48).

The other instance of people speaking in tongues is found in Acts 19:6. There were some people there who had believed the preaching of John the Baptist and yet had not heard about Jesus. When they heard about Jesus and were baptized, Paul laid hands on them and they received the Holy Spirit, spoke in tongues, and prophesied (Acts 19:1–6). Again, speaking in tongues served as an indication of the outpouring of the Holy Spirit on the people. It was not given here for the purpose of communicating to others in their own languages and so it differed from the day of Pentecost.

On the basis of these passages in Acts and certain other verses, Pentecostals and some Charismatics have formed a doctrine that claims speaking in tongues is the usual initial evidence of the Baptism in the Holy Spirit. Pentecostals believe that the Baptism in the Holy Spirit can occur at a time later than conversion and must be sought. Evangelicals disagree, claiming that every Christian has been baptized in the Holy Spirit (1 Cor 12:13) at regeneration and no sign of this event is necessary. As twenty-first-century western Christians, we are not accustomed to any manifestation of the Holy Spirit upon conversion. The occurrences recorded in Acts seem quite distant. Evangelicals in particular insist that believing in Christ is the evidence of having the Holy Spirit and no other sign is needed.

As a Charismatic, rather than a classical Pentecostal, I believe that the baptism in the Holy Spirit is not a second blessing, subsequent to conversion. But it is important for Christians not to take the presence of the Holy Spirit for granted. Sometimes we forget that the Holy Spirit is a divine person, who graciously indwells believers. We can fall into the trap of speaking of "it" and thinking about the Spirit as if he were some "thing." God has graciously poured out his Spirit on his people and we must continue to seek the fullness of the Spirit (Eph 5:18). Pentecostals have the right idea in seeking more of the Holy Spirit, instead of taking him for granted. But

1 Cor 12:30 implies that speaking in tongues cannot be for every person. "Do all possess gifts of healing? Do all speak with tongues? Do all interpret?" The Greek construction in this verse makes clear that the answer to these questions is intended to be No. So speaking in tongues cannot be the usual initial evidence of being baptized in the Holy Spirit. However, the gift appears quite common and should be sought out.

Paul observes in 1 Cor 13:8–10 that, although love continues for eternity, speaking in tongues will cease when the perfect comes. This passage has been used to insist that speaking in tongues is a temporary gift and has passed away because we have a complete canon, that is, a complete Bible. We no longer need speaking in tongues now, according to this argument. It is true that tongues and all other spiritual gifts are temporary. They are only for this age. In the age to come, when believers are raised from the dead and heaven comes to earth (Rev 21), there will be no need of spiritual gifts. However, it is false to insist that the gift of tongues has passed away because we now have the Bible. What is perfect will not come until Jesus has returned. Speaking in tongues was not an early church substitute for the Bible. It has a different function.

There are several instructions in 1 Cor 14 regarding the use of this gift. Of the gifts listed in 1 Cor 12:8–10, the only two gifts discussed at length are tongues and prophecy. They are contrasted in chapter 14. First of all, "For one who speaks in a tongue speaks not to men but to God; for no one understands him, but he utters mysteries in the Spirit" (1 Cor 14:2). For the most part, when someone speaks in tongues it is directed at God and not at other people. This makes it a great gift for praying. The statement "he utters mysteries in the Spirit" implies that speaking in tongues is not gibberish but something substantial. In the New Testament, "mystery" usually refers to the gospel or the kingdom of God (e.g., Matt 13:11; Rom 16:25; 1 Cor 2:7). It is a mystery that has been revealed with the coming of Jesus. So the person who speaks in tongues is in fact uttering words about the gospel, but they are unintelligible to the speaker and quite often to the hearers (the day of Pentecost was an exception). However, the mysteries about the gospel are actually edifying the inner being of the person speaking.

Because of this, "the one who speaks in a tongue builds up himself" (1 Cor 14:4). Therefore, speaking in tongues is contrasted with other gifts of the Spirit. All other gifts are given in order to edify others, but the gift of tongues is given to edify the one who has the gift. It can be used alone with no other purpose than to build up the speaker. The other gifts cannot be used in isolation since they are for the benefit of the body. Paul tells us,

"Now I want you all to speak in tongues" (1 Cor 14:5). This gift can and should be sought. God is generous and will give to those who ask him. It is not something shameful to want to speak in tongues, even though it does not benefit others. However, since it is a gift for personal benefit, it is not to be flaunted. There are ways to use it in congregational settings, but it is mainly for private use.

The purpose of using spiritual gifts in the congregation is to build up one another. But since speaking in tongues is generally unintelligible to speaker and hearer (1 Cor 14:9), it fails to fulfill this purpose (1 Cor 14:11) unless interpreted. Speaking in tongues is not a demonstration of spirituality; improper use may puff up the speaker and alienate the hearers, rather than build up the church. However, instructions are given for its use in congregational settings. Two significant actions demonstrate love: there should be interpretation and there should be order. "If any speak in a tongue, let there be only two or at most three, and each in turn, and let someone interpret. But if there is no one to interpret, let each of them keep silent in church and speak to himself and to God" (1 Cor 14:27–28). Unintelligible words are of no use to the congregation. That is why Paul instructs believers with this gift to pray for the ability to interpret what they say (1 Cor 14:13). Interpretation makes the speech intelligible and thus edifying to others. The speaker need not be the one who interprets. But if no one present can interpret, then the tongues-speakers must be quiet. Love also expresses itself in an orderly way. People need an opportunity to exercise their gifts in church, but it must not be a free-for-all. People should not all speak at once. Speaking in tongues is a helpful gift when used with others in mind.

Speaking in tongues has two possible audiences—humans and God. On the day of Pentecost the audience was human. In that case, the people who were listening to the tongues were unbelievers and the tongues acted as a sign pointing to the gospel, which was then proclaimed to them. In the case of church meetings, speaking in tongues is directed at encouraging the church, as long as an interpretation is given. In other instances, tongues are directed at God as praise or prayer. It is still speech and it is intelligible to God. Paul also mentions singing with the spirit (1 Cor 14:5), implying that it is possible to sing in tongues. This is speech delivered musically. The audience for singing in tongues must be God since it is worship. I don't imagine it would be translated for the congregation.

"So, my brothers, earnestly desire to prophesy, and do not forbid speaking in tongues" (1 Cor 14:39). Christians are exhorted to desire the gift of prophecy since prophecy is intelligible speech and therefore edifies the church. Edifying others is important, and yet Paul does not say, "Don't speak in tongues." He says the opposite—"do not forbid speaking in tongues." Given the way some churches avoid all consideration of this gift, the command must be headed. Tongues is not something to avoid but something to be gratefully used, as with other gifts of the Spirit. The Holy Spirit does not give the church gifts in order for them to be ignored or worse still treated as something bad. Speaking in tongues needs to find a place in church and be used appropriately.

There is one more instruction about speaking in tongues in 1 Cor 14. "Thus tongues are a sign not for believers but for unbelievers, while prophecy is a sign not for unbelievers but for believers" (1 Cor 14:22). Both prophecy and tongues act as a sign of judgment, the one on believers, and the other on unbelievers. The quotation in the previous verse is from Isa 28:11–12—"In the Law it is written, 'By people of strange tongues and by the lips of foreigners will I speak to this people, and even then they will not listen to me, says the Lord'" (1 Cor 14:21). The context of the Isaiah passage is the exile of Israel. Israel was in exile because they were under God's judgment. There they had to listen to strange languages, but they did not listen to God. So Paul applies this to unbelievers. When they come into the church and hear someone speaking in tongues, they will remain under the judgment of God because they will not understand the gospel mysteries being spoken. If they do not hear the gospel in their own language, they will be unable to come to repentance and accept the truth. Prophecy is also a sign of judgment since it convicts people of sin, and knowing they are under judgment they repent and are saved.

Speaking in tongues is a gift that is sometimes misunderstood and sometimes misused. But this gift and its counterpart, interpretation of tongues, are given as a blessing from God. They should not be maligned because despising a gift reflects poorly on the giver. Neither must they be used as a means of displaying spirituality. With proper use, the church will be uplifted as people speak in tongues and the tongues are interpreted. Although the gift is different to others, in that speaking in tongues edifies the speaker rather than the congregation, the Holy Spirit seems to give this gift to many. So Christians should feel free to pray for the gift of speaking in tongues, and those who want to use it in congregational settings should pray for the gift of interpretation.

21

Helping

"And God has appointed in the church first apostles, second prophets, third teachers, then miracles, then gifts of healing, *helping*, administrating, and various kinds of tongues" (1 Cor 12:28).

THE GIFT OF HELPING should not be underestimated. It is not a trivial gift. Helping others reflects the help that God gives his people. Israel's God is their helper; Jesus is the helper of the church; and the Holy Spirit helps the people of God in their weakness.

To understand the gift of helping we must begin in the Old Testament. Helping is commanded on a human level. "If your brother becomes poor and cannot maintain himself with you, you shall *support* him as though he were a stranger and a sojourner, and he shall live with you" (Lev 25:35). A failure to help others in need results in God's judgment. "Behold, this was the guilt of your sister Sodom: she and her daughters had pride, excess of food, and prosperous ease, but did not *aid* the poor and needy" (Ezek 16:49).

On a different level the helper of Israel is their God. "You have given me the shield of your salvation, and your right hand *supported* me, and your gentleness made me great" (Ps 18:35; see also Pss 22:19; 84:5; 89:18; 118:13). Frequently God helped Israel in battle (e.g., 1 Chr 12:18; 2 Chr 14:11; 25:8; 26:7). In Isa 41–50, the LORD is called the helper of Israel seven times. In multiple Psalms, God is mentioned as helper. He helps the fatherless against the wicked (Ps 10:14). He is the helper of those who call on him when they are distressed (Pss 28:7; 30:11; 33:20; 37:40; 46:1, 5). His help delivers people from the wicked (Ps 54:6). The poor are helped by him (Pss 70:5; 72:12–13). He helps the hungry, the sick, the oppressed, widows and orphans, and the alien (Ps 146:5–9).

The New Testament also speaks of God helping Israel. "He has helped his servant Israel, in remembrance of his mercy" (Luke 1:54). This is part of the *Magnificat*, which Mary sang while pregnant with Jesus. How has the LORD helped Israel? He did so by sending his Son into the world as God made flesh in the womb of a virgin. He has come to us as Immanuel. This is the help God gives to his people. As God with us, Jesus also acted as the helper of Israel. Compare this description of God in Ps 146 with the ministry of Jesus. "Blessed is he whose help is the God of Jacob, whose hope is in the LORD his God, who made heaven and earth, the sea, and all that is in them, who keeps faith forever; who executes justice for the oppressed, who gives food to the hungry. The LORD sets the prisoners free; the LORD opens the eyes of the blind" (Ps 146:5–8a). Jesus was sent to "proclaim liberty to the captives and recovery of sight to the blind, to set at liberty those who are oppressed" (Luke 4:18b). Jesus came as the helper of Israel in the flesh.

Jesus is the helper of Israel, and by extension the church, in several ways. Just as God was Israel's helper in battle, Jesus helps his people in the spiritual battle. Through his death on the cross, he defeated the demonic forces that oppose us (Col 2:15). The help of God is always available in Christ. "For he says, 'In a favorable time I listened to you, and in a day of salvation I have helped you.' Behold, now is the favorable time; behold, now is the day of salvation" (2 Cor 6:2).

Jesus helps those who are being tested (Heb 2:18). He is the great high priest who has suffered and died, and is therefore is able to help others who are suffering. What kind of help does Jesus give to believers who are suffering? The answer to that lies in understanding what a high priest does. The high priest stands in the presence of God on behalf of the people. Jesus is at God's right hand and now intercedes for his people day and night (Rom 8:34). There are examples of Jesus interceding for his people in the Gospels. He prayed for his disciples and the church in John 17 (see also Luke 22:31–32).

The Holy Spirit is also our helper. "Likewise the Spirit helps us in our weakness. For we do not know what to pray for as we ought, but the Spirit himself intercedes for us with groanings too deep for words. And he who searches hearts knows what is the mind of the Spirit, because the Spirit intercedes for the saints according to the will of God" (Rom 8:26–27). The way in which the Spirit helps believers is through intercession. Since both Jesus and the Spirit help the church through their intercession, there is a good chance that intercession is part of the gift of helping. If so, then this explains why there is no specific mention of a gift of intercession in the New Testament, even though the gift is of great importance to the church.

Whether we consider intercession as a gift of the Spirit separate from helping, or whether it is part of the gift of helping, some passages in the epistles underscore its importance. "Epaphras, who is one of you, a servant of Christ Jesus, greets you, always struggling on your behalf in his prayers, that you may stand mature and fully assured in all the will of God" (Col 4:12). Every Christian is expected to pray and to intercede for others. But Epaphras went beyond the average in praying for others. It seems that he had a gift of intercession or a gift of helping. Epaphras was able to pray far more than do other people. He was indeed driven to pray constantly for the church to become mature. Intercession is a gift that is not often seen, but without it the church would not mature as it should. Struggling in prayer for the church is a major part of spiritual warfare. This connects intercession to the Old Testament declaration that the LORD is the helper of Israel in battle. Those with the gift of intercession call upon the God of our Lord Jesus Christ to help in spiritual battles.

Helping is a gift for both inside and outside the church. The church is called to help the weak (Acts 20:35). Those who are weak may include the poor, the sick, and the oppressed. Believers can receive help in these areas. However, many outside the church need help, and receiving this can enable them to see the gospel in action. The gift of helping as an expression of the gospel can involve delivering people from things that oppress and oppose them. This suggests that those called to help may fight against slavery or against poverty and economic oppression. There is much more to the gift of helping than doing menial tasks. This is a practical gift that enables Christians to help others out of their circumstances and into freedom and functionality. It may involve helping people get employment, helping people budget and get out of debt, freeing people from dependence on welfare, getting women out of sexual slavery by giving them skills to begin a business, enabling more functional relationships, strengthening marriages, or mentoring.

The gift of helping is grounded in the help God gives his people. It was expressed in the life of Jesus as he helped people out of their bondage, sickness, and oppression. It is continually expressed by Jesus and the Holy Spirit as they intercede for the people of God. Helping is a practical gift that enables people to be freed from what holds them back, such as debt, slavery, oppression, and dysfunctional behavior. The practical work is accompanied by intercession for people. The two aspects of the gift can work in concert.

22

Administration/Guidance

"And God has appointed in the church first apostles, second prophets, third teachers, then miracles, then gifts of healing, helping, *administrating*, and various kinds of tongues" (1 Cor 12:28).

WHAT IS OFTEN TRANSLATED as the gift of administration is better translated as the gift of directing or guiding. The word used in 1 Cor 12:28 is rare in the Bible. However, the meaning is clear. This word, and others like it, is used in relation to the pilot of a ship, the helmsman, or the captain. The English word "administration" has more to do with forms and organization. For most of my Bible-reading life I associated this gift with the church secretary. But this is not what it means. The gift of administration is about leading the church in the right direction. It is about piloting the church. Just as the captain of the ship was charged with being aware of the time of year, the stars, the winds, and the tides, so the person who is gifted with administration must be aware of all the things that will affect the church.

The word is used three times in the Septuagint (second-century BC Greek translation of the Old Testament). There it is used to mean "wise guidance" or "clever direction." "Let the wise hear and increase in learning, and the one who understands obtain *guidance*" (Prov 1:5). "Where there is no *guidance*, a people falls, but in an abundance of counselors there is safety" (Prov 11:14). "For by wise *guidance* you can wage your war, and in abundance of counselors there is victory" (Prov 24:6). Wise guidance is necessary so that people are able to behave in a godly way. People fall without guidance. They do not do what is right, because they become confused and lost. Guidance allows wars to be successfully fought. Otherwise nothing effective is accomplished. This is true of churches. No matter how many gifts are given to the church, someone needs to direct their use so that God's purposes are accomplished. People will simply flounder around without guidance. The church will be utterly ineffective in its purpose if there is no pilot at the helm.

The New Testament does not call Jesus the pilot of the church, but the early church did use this image. "The sea is the world in which the church is surrounded by storms like a ship on the sea, but it does not founder because it has on board the experienced pilot, Christ."[1] There are allusions to this idea in other early Christian writings. The symbolism is that Jesus is the pilot who steers the church through the storms of life and perils of sin and takes them to safety.

The two gifts of leading/pastoring and administration/guidance are likely to be related to one another, but they are not the same. Pastoring is concerned with meeting the spiritual needs of the church and administration/guidance is concerned with giving direction to the church.

1. Hippolytus of Rome, *De Antichristo* 59

Conclusion

THE AIM OF THIS study was to answer a number of questions about spiritual gifts. Having carefully explored the meaning and use of the gifts in the New Testament, I have arrived at some general conclusions. I have endeavored throughout the book to consider how the gifts of the Spirit operated in the life of Jesus. He ministered in the power of the Spirit in order to meet the needs of humanity. His ministry was a demonstration of God's compassion and love for human beings, who are lost and in desperate need of help. The church is charged with carrying on the ministry of Jesus.

Jesus did not leave his church to deal with the overwhelming needs of humanity in their own abilities. This would have been a catastrophic failure. If the church acts in its own ability, it is as if Jesus had never come into the world. But it does not have to be this way. Jesus has increased the sphere of his ministry by equipping the church with the gifts of the Spirit. Because of this, the church can carry on the ministry of Jesus to the whole world.

But the church has not yet reached "the measure of the stature of the fullness of Christ" (Eph 4:13b). For this reason, the gifts of the Spirit have been given first to build up the church. As the church is matured and built up, it is enabled to take the gospel out into the world. There, the gospel can be proclaimed to hurting human beings, not just in words but also in deeds, ranging from feeding the hungry, to healing the physically sick, to reconciling enemies, and to releasing people from oppression.

The gifts of the Spirit are not optional extras for the church. Without them we cannot effectively bring the gospel to the world. Without spiritual gifts, the church will neither know the fullness of Christ nor be able to offer Christ effectively to the lost. If the gifts of the Spirit are lacking in the church, then it is time that we sought the God who gives them. We know that he is good and merciful. "If you then, who are evil, know how to give good gifts to your children, how much more will the heavenly Father give the Holy Spirit to those who ask him!" (Luke 11:13). So let us ask him.

www.ingramcontent.com/pod-product-compliance
Lightning Source LLC
Chambersburg PA
CBHW060359090426
42734CB00011B/2189